Letters from the Father's Heart

Zach Bolt

Unless otherwise indicated, all Scripture quotations are taken from *The Holy Bible: New International Version*. Copyright © 1973, 1978, 1984 by The International Bible Society. Used by permission of Zondervan Bible Publishers.

All Scripture quotations marked NKJV are taken from the *New King James Version* of the Bible. Copyright © 1979, 1980, 1982, 1994, Thomas Nelson, Inc., Publishers.

Letters from the Father's Heart
ISBN: 0-88144-306-9

Published by
Thorncrown Publishing
A Division of Yorkshire Publishing Group
7707 East 111th Street, Suite 104
Tulsa, OK 74133
www.yorkshirepublishing.com

DEAR READER,

The most important thing for you to understand as you read this book is how much your Heavenly Daddy loves you. He longs for an intimate relationship with you beyond anything you could ever imagine. The work that you hold in your hands represents not only more than a year of my life, but also more than a decade of struggles and trials as I personally endeavored to mature in Christ. You have been in my heart and prayers through the late nights, the long days, and the weekends as I have tried to balance writing this book with working a full time job, a marriage, serving in ministry, and a little personal time.

After I gave my life to the Lord I became really hungry for a personal relationship with Him. I also struggled mightily with fear and depression for a number of years. As I was diligent to seek the Lord, He not only showed me how to enter into an intimate relationship with Him, but He also showed me how to walk in victory over the works of the enemy that had held me bound. I know that my desires and my struggles are not unique, but rather are common to countless multitudes of others. The names and faces change, but all over the world there are people who are hungry for God and struggle daily in their Christian walk.

I wrote this book at a direct leading from the Father. It includes principles and teaching I have gained from countless hours in prayer and study of the Word, and that I have compiled into a series of letters written as though from God the Father. These letters will introduce you into how I know my Heavenly Father and how I interact with Him daily. The material in this book is how I now live in victory rather than defeat as in the past. I am a very simple person, and this is what works for me. If you will apply these principles and teachings to your life, they will work for you, too.

I remember in those early days how I was so hungry for God that I would have done anything to have a rich, personal relationship with Him, but I just did not know how. I would have done anything to be free from the chains of bondage, but no one seemed able to help me. I wish that I would have had someone to tell me years ago the things that are written in this book so that I could have begun living in victory long before I did. I used to hold on to the verse where Paul says that the Father comforts us in all tribulation so that we may comfort others who are suffering, as well. I used to think to myself that one day I would be able to comfort others who were suffering the same and similar things that I was suffering. It is my prayer that this book, which I have poured my life into, will comfort and console you and bring you freedom like you have never known.

I love you with the love of the Lord!

In His Hands,

Zach Bolt

DEDICATION

This book is dedicated to my Heavenly Daddy,
Who daily holds me by the hand,
to my friend, the Holy Spirit,
Who is my constant companion,
and to my Lord and Savior Jesus, Who is my all in all.
You guys are the best!

Also, this book is dedicated to my beautiful wife,
who has encouraged me every step of the way.
Honey, I would be lost without you.
And to my family, who has always been there for me.
I love you guys.

Finally, I dedicate this book to every single person
whose life will be changed by reading it.
May your struggles cease, and may you come to
know God as your Daddy, Who holds you by the hand.

CONTENTS

Dearest Precious ______________________________,
(your name here)

I love you! Your Father in Heaven loves you more than you could ever imagine. You are the joy and rejoicing of My heart, and I delight in you endlessly.

Little one, please take a minute to look around at the beautiful world I have created: the flowers, the trees, the sun, the animals, everything. I have so carefully crafted every single thing on earth including you. Look at the wonder of your own body. Move your hands and see how wonderfully you are made. You are an amazing creation, and I know everything about you down to the smallest detail. I know how many hairs you have on your head right now. I even know how many cells are in your body! My eyes are always on you, and I am intimately concerned with every minute detail of your life. You are unique, special; there is no one else like you on earth.

I created you for a specific purpose. I laid out a plan for your life before you were ever born. My plan is good; one that will bring you happiness and contentment. It pleases Me greatly to see your life prosper and flourish in every way!

My child, you cannot see Me, but you can still know Me. I am always with you, and I will never leave you, even for a second. I wrote the Bible for you so that you can truly know Me and My plan for your life. It includes everything you could possibly need to know about Me and living your life in the blessing that I intended. I have left absolutely nothing out.

I am going to write you a series of letters that will help you in your walk with Me. Following this introductory letter will be thirty-four other letters. They will cover the five major areas of your life:

- Your relationship with Me,
- Your relationship with your family,
- Your relationships with others,
- Kingdom principles, and
- Your personal development.

These letters are designed to help you understand My heart, and give you examples of how to apply My Word to your daily life. I want these letters to be very real and personal to you, so put your name on the blank line at the beginning of every letter. At the end of each letter I will give you some verses from My Word that apply to the topic of the letter. Meditate on these verses, and allow the water of My Word to soak into the soil of your heart.

Following the verses, you will find some questions that will require you to search your heart for the answers. I have also written a prayer that you can pray back to Me in response to what I have written to you. Finally, you will find a section at the end of the prayer called "Identifying with My Father," where I have provided you with a single thought for further meditation followed by a space for you to write your own thoughts. Through these channels, we can have a living interaction as your faith and our relationship grows stronger day by day.

Dearest child, if you could see Me with your eyes and touch Me with your hands, imagine what our relationship would be like then. You would always be consciously aware of My presence. I would be your constant companion, and we would walk and talk together all the time.

Even though I am not visible to you, we can still enjoy a rich fellowship in the Spirit. As you read these letters, I want you to picture Me right there with you, hugging you close, laughing with you, and wiping away your tears. Picture Me, your loving Daddy, speaking to you the things that are written in these letters. This is My heart. Be free, My love, as you read these letters from My heart to yours. I love you with an everlasting love!

Love,

Dad

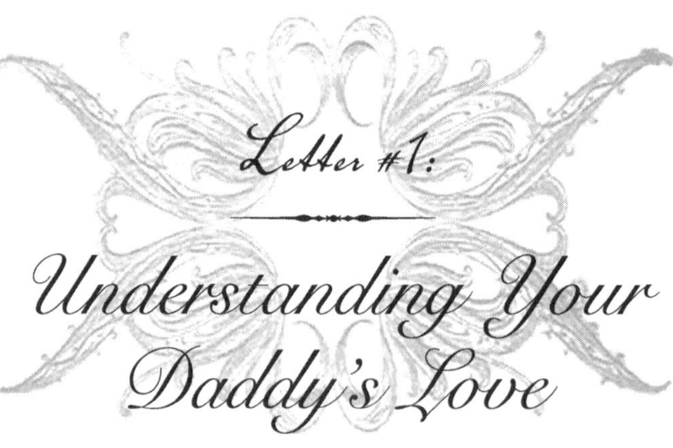

Letter #1:

Understanding Your Daddy's Love

Dearest ________________________________,

(your name here)

Oh, I love you so very much! You are My special child. Please come, let Me hug you and hold you in My arms as I tell you all about My love for you. My child, this first letter is the most important because a revelation of My love is the foundation to the fullness of life that I have planned for you.

Just like a loving earthly parent, I wanted a precious child I could love. I needed a loving relationship so I created you, and you are the apple of My eye. I made a special place inside you that only a loving relationship with Me can satisfy. There is also a place inside Me that only a loving relationship with you can satisfy. Just as a child and its loving parents cry out for each other, so our hearts cry out for each other, too. This yearning causes us to want to be together, and in being together in harmony we are both fulfilled.

When sin entered the world, I was cut off from the people I loved so very dearly. My heart was broken. My precious ones that I created to love and fellowship with were utterly lost, and I had to do something about it. The only thing I could do was send My precious Son Jesus to die on a cross to restore our relationship. Your big brother, Jesus, willingly gave His life so that you and I could be restored to fellowship and intimacy. If you had been the only person on earth who needed salvation, Jesus still would have died just for you! My love, can you see how special you are to Me?!

My child, I love you beyond your ability to understand or comprehend. If My love were a mountain, Mt. Everest would look like an anthill beside it!! If My love were an ocean, all the waters of the world would look like a drop in a bucket in comparison!! I love you! Every morning when the sun rises, I am saying, "I love you." Every time the wind kisses your face, I am saying, "I love you." I am everywhere, in everything, and I am always whispering, speaking, shouting that "I LOVE YOU!!!!"

Love is not something that I have. Love is not something that I do. Love is what I am! I am love! I am love! I AM LOVE! Let's go to 1 Corinthians 13:4-8 and look at My definition of love. Everywhere you see the word "love" in these verses, you can put My name there. Daddy is patient. Daddy is kind. Daddy is love! I will never, ever say or do anything that is not based in love. No matter what the situation or circumstance, I will always act and respond to you in love. I will never do anything that is outside of My Word's definition of love found here in 1 Corinthians 13. Nothing! Never!

Little one, it breaks My heart to hear people speak untruths to you and mislead you about Me. I am broken when people tell you that I did things that I would never do, or that I said things that I would never say. Bless your heart, let Me hug you and hold you close. Together let's unlearn anything that you have been taught about Me that does not fit My nature as revealed to you in My Word.

Precious one, nothing would please Me more than to reveal My true self to you. Please let Me lavish My love on you, and wash away all fear and misunderstanding that have been sown into your heart. I love you very dearly, and I want us to share a precious, unhindered relationship. When you have questions and things you don't understand, please run to Me, because I am always here to guide you into the truth. You don't ever have to fear Me, because My perfect love casts out fear.

My child, as you learn My true nature, we will share a more intimate and fulfilling relationship than you have ever imagined. I love you, dearest heart.

Love,

Daddy

Words from the Father's Heart

John 3:16—"For God (Daddy) so loved the world that he gave his one and only Son, that whoever believes in him shall not perish but have eternal life."

1 Corinthians 13:4-8—"Love (Daddy) is patient, love (Daddy) is kind. It (He) does not envy, it (He) does not boast, it (He) is not proud. It (He) is not rude, it (He) is not self-seeking, it (He) is not easily angered, it (He) keeps no record of wrongs. Love (Daddy) does not delight in evil but rejoices with the truth. It

(He) always protects, always trusts, always hopes, always perseveres. Love (Daddy) never fails. . . ."

1 John 4:9-10—"This is how God (Daddy) showed his love among us: He sent his one and only Son into the world that we might live through him. This is love: not that we loved God (Daddy), but that he loved us and sent his Son as an atoning sacrifice for our sins."

1 John 4:16—"And so we know and rely on the love God (Daddy) has for us. God (Daddy) is love. Whoever lives in love lives in God (Daddy), and God (Daddy) in him."

Jeremiah 31:3—"The LORD (Daddy) appeared to us in the past, saying: 'I have loved you with an everlasting love; I have drawn you with loving-kindness.'"

1 John 3:1—"How great is the love the Father (Daddy) has lavished on us, that we should be called children of God (Daddy)! And that is what we are!"

Psalm 17:8—"Keep me as the apple of your eye. . . ."

Questions from the Father's Heart

1) Dearest child, after reading this letter and meditating on the Scriptures above, what things have you been taught about Me and My love that are not true in the light of My nature as revealed to you in My Word?

___

___

___

2) Name the qualities of My love for you, dear child, as given in 1 Corinthians 13:4-8:

3) My child, how will this new revelation of My love for you impact your relationship with Me?

4) How will you apply these new thoughts and ideas about My love to your everyday life and thinking?

Prayer to the Father

Daddy,

Thank You so much for Your love for me. Thank You, Jesus, for dying on the cross to save me and bring me into a close relationship with Daddy God. Thank You, Daddy, for always dealing with me in love. I have been taught things about You and Your love that are not true according to Your Word. Please help me to unlearn and forget anything I have believed about You that is wrong. Daddy, please continue to reveal Your heart and Your wonderful love to me so that we can share the relationship You have planned for us. I love You, Daddy!!! In Jesus' name I pray!

Love,

____

Identifying with My Father

Example: I am the apple of my Heavenly Daddy's eye.

(Now, add your own thoughts.)

____

____

____

____

____

____

____

Letter #2: Following After Daddy

Dearest ________________________________,

(your name here)

My child, come and let Me hold you. Please sit in My lap and let's enjoy being close for a few minutes. Rest in My love, and let Me bring you peace as you have never known.

Dear heart, I know you have been confused at times about how to follow Me, your Daddy, in everyday life. Well-meaning people have told you that you need to have a relationship with Me, but for the most part they have never told you how. You have been told that a relationship with Me is going to church or being a good person. Other people have said that you need to read your Bible and pray every day. The enemy has also whispered his lies to confuse you and make you feel like a failure.

You have been left asking yourself the question, "How do I truly follow my Father God like He desires?" My child, I have seen all your tears and your struggles, and I have heard your prayers asking Me to help you follow Me faithfully. Please let Me dry all your tears and wipe away all the sorrow that you have suffered as I reveal My plan to you. Today I am going to teach you in the simplest way how to follow Me.

As you sit in My lap, little one, imagine being alone with Me in your favorite quiet spot. Picture yourself as a little child about four years old. Now, based on what you learned about My love for you in the first letter, see Me there with you as your loving Daddy. Hold your hand out for Me to take it in Mine just as an earthly daddy takes his little child's hand. Follow Me hand in hand, My child, and I will lead, guide, and direct your steps in My righteous paths. Every day is a step in your journey through life. My child, this is how I have called you to follow after Me—not running behind or struggling to keep up, but hand in hand in a loving relationship.

My dear child, treasure this vision in your heart. This is the relationship that I desire to share with you daily. I am always with you to share in this intimate Father-child relationship. Please begin to apply this vision to your life and share in this relationship with Me every day. I long to spend time with you daily. I promise I will lead you by My Spirit. You are not a failure! You are My precious child, and you are able to follow after Me exactly as I desire. I love you, dear heart, and I will never let you fall.

Love,

Daddy

Words from the Father's Heart

Psalm 17:5, 16:11—"My steps have held to your paths; my feet have not slipped . . . You have made known to me the path of life; you will fill me with joy in your presence, with eternal pleasures at your right hand."

Psalm 32:8—"I will instruct you and teach you in the way you should go; I will counsel you and watch over you."

Psalm 37:23 NKJV—"The steps of a good man are ordered by the Lord (Daddy), and He delights in his way."

2 Corinthians 2:14—"But thanks be to God (Daddy), who always leads us in triumphal procession in Christ and through us spreads everywhere the fragrance of the knowledge of him."

Psalm 23:1-3—"The LORD (Daddy) is my shepherd, I shall not be in want. He makes me lie down in green pastures, he leads me beside quiet waters, he restores my soul. He guides me in paths of righteousness for his name's sake."

Questions from the Father's Heart

1) How did you picture your relationship with Me, your Heavenly Father, before reading this letter? ____________

____

____

____

____

____

____

____

2) My child, what new ideas have you learned in this letter that will positively influence our fellowship and interaction? ____________________________

3) What kind of relationship does your heart long to share with Me? ____________________________

4) Has this letter changed your view of our relationship? ____

How? ____________________________

5) How will you begin to apply the vision I have given you to your everyday life? ____________________________

PRAYER TO THE FATHER

Daddy,

I know that You have seen all my struggles in desiring an intimate relationship with You. I truly desire to follow after You according to Your plan. Thank You so much for being concerned about me and loving me. Thank You for this vision of wonderful fellowship that You have given to me. Right now I put my hand in Yours to begin following after You the way You have shown me. As I begin to apply this to my life every day, please make Yourself more real to me than ever before. Please lead me, guide me, and direct me as I walk with You. In Jesus' name I pray.

Love,

____

IDENTIFYING WITH MY FATHER

My Daddy orders, leads, guides, and directs my steps by the Holy Spirit. *(Now, add your own thoughts.)*

Letter #3: Fellowshipping with Daddy

Dearest ______________________________,

(your name here)

I love you so very much, dear heart. As I wrote the last letter, I rejoiced to begin sharing with you how to truly follow after Me. If you will continue to apply the principles I have begun teaching you, then all struggle in your relationship with Me will begin to disappear. Please come sit with Me again today, precious heart, and let Me teach you more about sharing a relationship with Me, your loving Daddy God. Today's letter is going to focus on teaching you about fellowship with Me.

Dearest child, I did not create you to be a robot. I do not expect you to blindly follow My orders and do exactly as you are told with no questions asked. What fun would that be for either of us? The cry of My heart is for you and Me to share a loving, intimate relationship that brings satisfaction to us both. I can see into your heart, and I know this is what you have yearned for, as well. Today I am going to teach you how to have your heart's desire.

In the natural there are basically two types of fellowship between a loving father and his dear child. I know you are asking Me, "Daddy, what do You mean?" Little one, please let Me explain. First, there is fellowship where father and child spend intimate time together. By this I mean that there are no outside distractions and they are focused on only one thing, each other. Sometimes they talk and share hearts, and at other times they may just sit quietly and enjoy being together. Let's call this intimate fellowship. The second kind of fellowship that I call casual fellowship is different. This is where father and child talk, laugh, joke, and just generally enjoy being together as they interact throughout the day while doing other tasks.

In a healthy relationship, both of these types of fellowship are very important. A loving father and child wouldn't think of not talking to each other at all throughout the day, nor would they never spend close personal time together. Both types of fellowship contribute to a close, healthy relationship. If there is one without the other, then the relationship will be out of balance. In the same way, as your Heavenly Daddy, I desire for us to share in both types of fellowship. It is important to your spiritual health and to our relationship that you stop and take time for intimate fellowship with Me every day. When you stop and spend time with Me, you allow Me to refresh you and speak to you in ways that you are not as able to receive in the busyness of your day. When you spend time with Me, I am able to renew your strength and give you rest.

Child, you are a branch, and I am the strong vine. If you are cut off from Me, you will not be able to be truly successful by My definition at anything. In order to stay fresh and alive, you must stay plugged into close, intimate fellowship with Me. I will keep you rooted firmly, for I am your strength.

It is equally important for you to spend time with Me in casual fellowship as you go about your day. This type of fellowship enables you to focus minute by minute on the One who is your strength and your source. Casual fellowship adds so much richness to any natural relationship, and the same is true of our relationship, as well. To be honest, if one of My dear children just spends time with Me for a little while and then goes off about their day and ignores Me, it really hurts My feelings. How do you think an earthly father would feel if his small child, whom he adores, spent time with him one-on-one for a bit and then completely ignored him for the rest of the day? I feel the same way when My kids do that to Me.

Dearest heart, I know you are eager to have this fellowship with Me that I have described here, and you are wondering how to begin. Do you remember the vision of you and Me together in the last letter? That is our starting point. Every morning when you wake up, I am right there to hug you, tell you I love you, and grab your hand to lead you through your day. All day, every day, I am right there holding you by the hand. If you will trust Me, I will direct every single one of your steps. I am always there to hug and hold you. I am ready for fellowship at any time during the day or night. Precious heart, do you see how simple this casual fellowship is?

Now, how do we fellowship intimately? Picture us together again in your favorite quiet spot. Now, let's find a nice place to sit down together. You can sit right in My lap, on My knee, or beside Me if you want. Now let's just spend time together. Talk to Me, and I will talk right back to you. Tell Me what's on your mind. Tell Me anything that is troubling you. You can ask for My guidance and direction, little one; I will gladly give it to you. If you need to cry, I will hold you. If you need love, I have plenty. If you just want a hug, it would be My pleasure.

Not only can we just enjoy talking and being together, but I will also help you dig deep into the riches of My Word. I have so many wonderful things to share with you that you can't even begin to imagine. I have hidden great riches in the pages of My Word for you and Me to discover together.

Dearest child, please take what I have written in this letter and begin to share in fellowship with Me. I am always right here longing to spend time with you, My love. You are so special to Me, and I desire to be with you. As you spend time with Me, I will reveal Myself to you in ways beyond your imagination. I love you, and I am always with you.

Love,

Daddy

WORDS FROM THE FATHER'S HEART

John 15:4-5—"Remain in me, and I will remain in you. No branch can bear fruit by itself; it must remain in the vine. Neither can you bear fruit unless you remain in me. I am the vine; you are the branches. If a man remains in me and I in him, he will bear much fruit; apart from me you can do nothing."

Psalm 34:10b—"Those who seek the LORD (Daddy) lack no good thing."

Deuteronomy 4:29—"But if from there you seek the LORD your God (Daddy), you will find him if you look for him with all your heart and with all your soul."

Psalm 63:1-8—"O God (Daddy), you are my God (Daddy), earnestly I seek you; my soul thirsts for you, my body longs for you, in a dry and weary land where there is no water. I have seen you in the sanctuary and beheld your power and your glory. Because your love is better than life, my lips will glorify you. I will praise you as long as I live, and in your name I will lift up my hands. My soul will be satisfied as with the richest of foods; with singing lips my mouth will praise you. On my bed I remember you; I think of you through the watches of the night. Because you are my help, I sing in the shadow of your wings. My soul clings to you; your right hand upholds me."

Isaiah 40:29-31—"He (Daddy) gives strength to the weary and increases the power of the weak. Even youths grow tired and weary, and young men stumble and fall; but those who hope in the LORD (Daddy) will renew their strength. They will soar on wings like eagles; they will run and not grow weary, they will walk and not be faint."

Questions from the Father's Heart

1) What struggles and roadblocks have you had in your relationship with Me?______________________________

2) How have these obstacles affected your ability to fellowship with Me as I have described in this letter?

3) How will you begin to practice both "intimate" and "casual" fellowship with Me daily?

4) How do you think enjoying these kinds of fellowship with Me regularly will change your life and our relationship?

Prayer to the Father

Daddy,

In the past I have struggled to understand how to relate to You and fellowship with You like my heart has desired. Thank You for loving me and revealing Yourself to me in a way that I have never known. I want to truly know You as my Daddy—Someone I can run to when I just feel the need to be close. I want to truly know Your heart and recognize Your presence with me at all times. I determine right now to begin spending time with You just learning how to have real relationship with You. I'm not sure I know how to do this, so I trust You to lead me, guide me, and show me how. I love You, Dad! In Jesus' name I pray.

Love,

____

Identifying with My Father

I am a branch attached to my Lord Jesus, the strong Vine.

(Now, add your own thoughts.)

Letter #4: Hearing Daddy's Voice

Dearest ________________________________,

(your name here)

You are the song of My heart, My greatest love. My child, in previous letters I have taught you many principles about relationship with Me. I have mentioned speaking to you as well as hearing My voice, but up to now I have not gone into any great detail concerning these areas. In this letter I want to specifically address the ways that I speak to you and teach you how to develop your spiritual ears so that you can hear Me clearly.

Dearest heart, I have been teaching you that a true relationship with your Daddy God is not nearly as difficult as you have thought. The same is true for hearing My voice speaking to you. Let Me ask you a question. Is it hard for a child to hear his earthly Daddy's voice speaking to him? No, of course not! Confusion and misunderstanding have made it hard for you to hear from Me, but today I am going to bring you clarity like never before.

Precious heart, there are three basic ways that your Heavenly Father will speak to you. First of all, *I will speak to you through My Word.* I have written My Word to give you something physical to grasp in reaching out to touch Me and find My heart. My Word is alive, and you have My precious Holy Spirit inside you to make it come alive in your heart. He will reveal My heart to you through My Word and make it explode inside you like a bomb of revelation. My Word reveals My heart and My will; it contains relevant wisdom and instruction for every situation you will ever face.

My child, the second way I will speak to you is *through My Holy Spirit in your heart.* He is your Companion and your Guide. My Word has many instructions and contains wisdom for every situation of your life, but sometimes the wisdom you need will be specific instructions spoken to you by the Spirit. For example, He might say, "Dearest heart, go here. . . ." or "My child, do this or say that. . . ." My Word says that My Spirit inside you will teach you and speak to you the things you need to know. The Holy Spirit and My Word always work in perfect harmony. My Word will speak to you, and the Spirit will quicken it to your heart. My Spirit will speak to you and bring to your mind what My Word says. My Spirit will guide you into all truth, and He will never, ever speak anything to you that does not agree with My Word.

The third way that I will speak to you will be *through another person.* Dear heart, you are not alone in this world. There are many other people like you who have a heart after Me. These precious people are your brothers and sisters in Christ. Sometimes I will position one of them at a strategic place in your life and give them My words to speak to you. When they speak to you by My Spirit, their words will align perfectly with My written Word. When this happens, listen to the Spirit inside you to either confirm or deny that what they have said is from Me. If a person's words are from Me, then the Spirit and the Word will always agree with them. If they do not all three agree, then you can know that person did not speak words from My heart.

Dear heart, I have shown you three ways I will speak to you as you follow Me in life. Now I will give you an example to tie everything together. A loving earthly father and his small child converse and exchange words very easily. There is no struggle or fear. One speaks; the other listens and responds. Do you remember the vision that I gave you in the second letter where I began teaching you how to follow Me? In the relationship I showed you, how would you speak to Me? How would I speak to you? In the vision, we are right there together, very close. What if I were a real flesh and blood person? You could speak to Me like you would a loving earthly father, and I would speak right back to you from a heart full of love. Look up into My eyes now, dear child. I am your loving Heavenly Daddy, and when you speak I always listen and respond gently and lovingly.

My child, if you will hold this vision close and act on what I have taught you, then you will begin to hear My voice speaking to you like never before. I will speak through My Word, My Spirit, and others, but no matter what method I choose, I love you, and My words will always be gentle and kind. You are My precious child and I love you so very dearly.

Love,

Daddy

Words from the Father's Heart

Psalm 119:105—"Your word is a lamp to my feet and a light for my path."

2 Timothy 3:16-17—"All Scripture is God (Daddy)-breathed and is useful for teaching, rebuking, correcting and training in righteousness, so that the man of God (Daddy) may be thoroughly equipped for every good work."

Jeremiah 33:3—"Call to me and I will answer you and tell you great and unsearchable things you do not know."

Isaiah 30:21—"Whether you turn to the right or to the left, your ears will hear a voice behind you, saying, 'This is the way; walk in it.'"

John 14:16-17—"And I will ask the Father (Daddy), and he will give you another Counselor to be with you forever—the Spirit of truth. The world cannot accept him, because it neither sees him nor knows him. But you know him, for he lives with you and will be in you."

John 16:12-13—"I have much more to say to you, more than you can now bear. But when he, the Spirit of truth, comes, he will guide you into all truth."

Colossians 3:16—"Let the word of Christ dwell in you richly as you teach and admonish one another with all wisdom, and as you sing psalms, hymns and spiritual songs with gratitude in your hearts to God (Daddy)."

QUESTIONS FROM THE FATHER'S HEART

1) What mind-sets and beliefs have hindered you from hearing My voice? ______________________

____

____

____

____

2) How will the principles found in this letter help you to better hear Me speaking to you? ______________________

____

____

____

____

3) How will you apply the example of the father and child to your life so that you can more easily begin to hear Me speak to you? ______________________

____

____

____

____

4) Take some time now to listen. What do you hear Me saying to you right now? ______________________

____

____

____

____

Prayer to the Father

Daddy,

Thank You so much for revealing Your plan about speaking to me. I am amazed that You desire to guide me by Your Word and Your Spirit. Please help me to hear Your voice speaking to me just like a father speaking to his child. Help me to hear You speak to me through Your Word, Your Spirit, and through others, as well. I am listening, Daddy, and as I hear Your voice I will be obedient. In Jesus' name I pray.

Love,

____

Identifying with My Father

The Words of my Heavenly Daddy dwell in me richly.

(Now, add your own thoughts.)

____

____

____

____

____

____

____

____

____

Letter #5:

How to Stay Fresh and Focused

Dearest ______________________________,

(your name here)

I want you to know and truly experience My great love for you. I see all your movements, and I know your deepest thoughts. I even have the hairs on your head numbered. Nothing about your life escapes My notice, for I am infinitely concerned and acquainted with everything about you. My child, it troubles me when I see you burdened down with cares and wandering through life lacking purpose and direction.

The world can be a difficult place, and I see the responsibilities and the obligations that pull at you every day. There are so many things vying for your attention that it sometimes becomes difficult to know where to place your focus. Please allow Me, your Heavenly Daddy, to relieve you of those burdens you have been carrying. Let Me refresh and refocus you and teach you how to live life resting in My love.

The first step to regaining focus and being refreshed is to identify the root cause of your feelings that your life is spiraling out of control. Remember, your enemy is the god of this world and its system. The enemy has set this world's system up to get everyone, particularly My children, on a life-draining treadmill. If you are on a treadmill, what are you doing? You are running in place! Time passes and you work hard, but you don't get anywhere. You go and go and go and end up in the same place more weary than when you began. I call this the treadmill of life, and your enemy is a master at tricking people into getting on it.

Once he has you there, he keeps turning up the speed so you work harder but still don't get anywhere. His lie is that if you will just work harder, you will be able to get everything done and life will be perfect. He tells you that if you run just a little bit faster, soon you will be able to rest for a while. Unfortunately, the enemy is able to blind many people so that they can't even see what he is doing to them. They swallow his lie that they "have" to keep running. They believe that if they stop running, their whole life will come crashing down around them. Fear gets them on the treadmill and keeps them there.

Tired, unfocused people are ineffective people. Ineffective people do not change their world; they do not accomplish the things that I have called them to accomplish. Effective people, on the other hand, are focused and energetic. I am going to teach you today how to become focused and effective by showing you how to get off life's treadmill and start walking successfully with Me.

My child, do you remember the vision I gave you of us walking together? Using this vision, let's take a fresh look at Psalm 23. In this passage I promised to lead you beside quiet waters and to restore your soul. Imagine yourself with Me in the peaceful scene described in these verses, resting beside cool, refreshing waters. My Word is living water to your spirit man. As you spend quiet time with Me in My Word and in fellowship, I will completely restore and refresh your soul.

Consider your big brother, Jesus. The gospels record many instances where He withdrew from the crowds to be alone in prayer. He was taking much needed rest from His ministerial duties and allowing Me to renew and refocus Him. In the same way, a close relationship with Me will bring about renewal and focus for your life. As My child, you are redeemed from the world and its system, and you do not have to live your life on a treadmill. Let Me give you some practical advice on how to get out of the grind that has been draining the life out of you.

First, you must begin to take time out of your busy schedule to spend with Me daily. Doing so will strengthen your life-giving relationship with Me, and will allow Me to order your life and priorities. Next, allow Me to be Lord over your schedule, and I will see to it that you are never overloaded. I will show you ways to maximize your days so that you will always have plenty of time to do what needs to be done.

In My Word I said that I am your source. Visualize Me as a power outlet. When you plug a drill into an outlet, it receives the power it needs to drill a hole. When you pull the drill's plug, it is no longer able to work for you. The same is true with you. You are like a power tool, and I am the power outlet. If you keep yourself "plugged" into Me, then you will have all the power you need for your life, but if you get "unplugged" from My power, you will not be able to function properly. My child, get plugged into My power source and remain plugged in through daily fellowship with Me! I love you and I am always with you.

Love,

Daddy

WORDS FROM THE FATHER'S HEART

Psalm 27:14—"Wait for the LORD (Daddy); be strong and take heart and wait for the LORD (Daddy)."

Isaiah 40:31—"Those who hope in the LORD (Daddy) will renew their strength. They will soar on wings like eagles; they will run and not grow weary, they will walk and not be faint.

Psalm 23:1-3—"The LORD (Daddy) is my shepherd, I shall not be in want. He makes me lie down in green pastures, he leads me beside quiet waters, he restores my soul. He guides me in paths of righteousness for his name's sake."

Zephaniah 3:17—"The LORD your God (Daddy) is with you, he is mighty to save. He will take great delight in you, he will quiet you with his love, he will rejoice over you with singing."

Matthew 11:28-30—"Come to me, all you who are weary and burdened, and I will give you rest. Take my yoke upon you and learn from me, for I am gentle and humble in heart, and you will find rest for your souls. For my yoke is easy and my burden is light."

QUESTIONS FROM THE FATHER'S HEART

1) What things have caused you to be weary and out of focus? In other words, what has put you on life's treadmill? ____

2) Listen carefully to My Spirit. What do you hear Him telling you to eliminate from your life? ____________________

3) What is He guiding you to focus on as priorities? ________

4) What is your personal strategy to keep your life off the treadmill and focused on the things that I lead you to do?

Prayer to the Father

Daddy,

I have been so weary and out of focus. It seems that the cares of this world have weighed me down. I am sorry for getting on the treadmill of life and not listening carefully to Your Holy Spirit. As You direct my life, I will obey You. I will start letting You call the shots in my life. Right now, by faith, I step off life's treadmill. I refuse to walk to the beat of the world's drum. Please refresh and restore me according to Your Word. Please give me fresh focus. I choose to plug myself in to Your power supply from this day forward. My relationship with You comes first, and I will allow You to guide my life and its activities. I love you! In Jesus' name I pray!

Love,

Identifying with My Father

My Heavenly Daddy rejoices over me with singing.

(Now, add your own thoughts.)

Letter #6:

The Importance of the Word

My Precious Child ________________________,

(your name here)

I just want to tell you how much I love you, and how My heart rejoices in you. You are the apple of My eye, the center of all My attention. Here is a big hug from your Daddy! You can feel safe and sound here with Me, and you can rest knowing that nothing in this world can hurt you in any way, because your Daddy has you in His arms.

I am very excited today, because I am about to completely change your perception of My Word. You have heard and been taught many different things about My Word, because everyone has a different opinion about it. You have been told that it's a rule book and that I will "get you" if you don't obey it completely. You have been made to feel guilty for not reading it enough. In church you are told that you should hold fast to it in faith, no matter what! So exactly what are you supposed to believe about My Word? This letter will set the record straight so that you can begin to use My Word effectively to bring about the success that I desire for you.

My child, the first questions that must be answered are, "What is the purpose of My Word, and why did I write it for you?" You will never be able to understand and apply My Word to your life if you do not understand the purpose behind it! The Bible is a collection of letters that I wrote to guide you into the success and fullness that I have planned for you. It is not a dusty set of rules and regulations that I thought up just to complicate your life. I am not mad at you if you fail to follow every instruction to the letter. You must get that idea out of your head because I am your Daddy, and I love you.

Begin to see My Word not as a rule book but as a success manual that I designed to set you free and put your life on the Kingdom track. Think about this: I spent centuries inspiring dozens of men to write the Bible's sixty-six books. I did it just for you, My precious child, and I would still have done it even if I had known that you were the only person who was ever going to need it. This reveals My heart full of love for you!

Now, think back to the vision of us together as Father and child, and picture Me standing in front of you as your loving Heavenly Daddy. Visualize Me handing your Bible to you and saying, "Here are My words written just for you. Read them and believe them with all your heart, My child. Every word was put there for your success, because I want you to prosper in every area of your life. I know you have struggled at times to truly believe My Word. You have said to yourself, *How can I ever walk in true faith? How can I truly believe for what the Word says to manifest in my life?* Child, the answer is simple. I am standing before you, and I am telling you that you can believe everything I have written for you. You can confidently place your complete trust in Me, for I will never break your trust nor will I ever let you down. As you place your complete trust in Me and in My Word, I will do exceedingly abundantly above all you can ask or imagine so that your faith in Me will continue to grow unhindered."

I have a question for you, and I want you to imagine that you are looking directly into My eyes and answer it. "Have I spoken anything in My Word that I will not do?" I know your heart and I know your answer to this question, but I want you to come face-to-face with what you truly believe.

Let Me give you an image of My Word that will redefine the way you walk through life. I want you to imagine a Bible taller than you standing open in front of you. Visualize it so large in your mind that you can't see over it or around it. Look down and imagine it open and just as large under your feet. See it open to the promise that addresses your situation. Now, instead of being confronted with problems and circumstances, you are confronted with My Word concerning your life. Focusing on My Word instead of the problems brings My deliverance on the scene for you. By remembering this simple example you will be better equipped to be grounded on the rock of My Word instead of being blown about by the storms of life.

Meditate on My Word and let it become part of you; it will prepare you to meet life's challenges with success. Put it in your heart and in your mouth and continue to believe it and speak it because it is true, no matter what you see with your eyes. Rest confidently in My love and in My ability. I love you and I will never ever let you fall.

Love,

Dad

WORDS FROM THE FATHER'S HEART

Isaiah 55:10-11—"As the rain and the snow come down from heaven, and do not return to it without watering the earth and making it bud and flourish, so that it yields seed for the sower and bread for the eater, so is my word that goes out from my mouth: It will not return to me empty, but will accomplish what I desire and achieve the purpose for which I sent it."

Psalm 119:89—"Your word, O LORD (Daddy), is eternal; it stands firm in the heavens."

Psalm 119:105—"Your word is a lamp to my feet and a light for my path."

John 6:63—"The Spirit gives life; the flesh counts for nothing. The words I have spoken to you are spirit and they are life."

Numbers 23:19—"God (Daddy) is not a man, that he should lie, nor a son of man, that he should change his mind. Does he speak and then not act? Does he promise and not fulfill?"

Joshua 1:8—"Do not let this Book of the Law depart from your mouth; meditate on it day and night, so that you may be careful to do everything written in it. Then you will be prosperous and successful."

2 Timothy 3:16-17—"All Scripture is God (Daddy)-breathed and is useful for teaching, rebuking, correcting and training in righteousness, so that the man of God (Daddy) may be thoroughly equipped for every good work."

Questions from the Father's Heart

1) Take a few minutes to think about how you have truly seen My Word. Write down these perceptions that you have carried up until now. ______________________________
____
____
____
____
____

2) How has My letter helped you to see My Word differently than you did before? ______________________________
____
____
____
____
____

3) How do the examples that I gave you in this letter impact your ability to trust and believe Me and My Word?
____
____

4) How do you plan to incorporate what I have taught you into your daily life? ______

PRAYER TO THE FATHER

Daddy,

I realize that I have had misconceptions about Your Word. Please forgive me. I give them all to You. Thank You so much for writing the Bible just for me. I receive Your Word as though You were standing in front of me and handing it to me as a gift. With Your help I will read it, believe it, speak it, and act on it, no matter what I see. Please help me to put Your Word before my eyes and focus on it in all situations just like You have taught me. Your Word is a lamp to my feet and a light to my path. Please place a hunger in me for Your Word like never before. I love You. In Jesus' name I pray.

Love,

______

Identifying with My Father

My Heavenly Daddy's Word is a success manual for me, and I delight in meditating on it daily.

(Now, add your own thoughts.)

Letter #7:
The Gift of Family

Dear ______________________________,

(your name here)

I love you, My blessed child. Today's letter shifts the focus from your relationship with Me to your relationship with your family. Family is My divine institution, and if you will follow My plan for your family, you will be blessed and prosperous in your relationships.

Family is not man's idea, it's My idea. In the beginning, I created man to need a companion and a helper, and when I created Eve to complete Adam, the first family was formed. I designed a bond called marriage to join a man and a woman in a permanent covenant relationship. I created this covenant to be the foundation of the family and all its relationships.

I designed the family to be a model of My relationship with people on earth. When sin entered the world, man not only lost fellowship with Me, but the family unit fell into chaos, as well. I have gone to great lengths to restore both My relationship with humanity as well as mankind's family relationships. This restoration was not an easy task, but now in Christ you are restored to perfect fellowship with Me, and you can also enjoy the total restoration of your family to the perfection of My original design.

My child, in order for your family order to be restored and whole, you must be willing to do what it takes to bring about peace and harmony. I have been teaching you how to relate to Me as your Father, because everything successful in your life will begin with a successful relationship with Me. Please continue to allow My Holy Spirit to build upon the principles of relationship with Me that I have been teaching you. As you grow in your relationship with Me, you will be empowered by the Spirit to bring your family relationships in line with My Word.

After building the foundation of your life on relationship with Me, then we can go to My Word and learn how the family is supposed to operate. Once you begin to learn these principles, you will be able to apply your belief in My Word to seeing your family become what My Word says that it should be. I do not expect you to accomplish this in your own strength, but you have the Holy Spirit inside you to help you. My child, the surest way to lead your family in the right direction is for you to start fulfilling your role as revealed in My Word. When you do, others will begin to see the change in your life. Your obedience to My Word gives the Holy Spirit greater entrance into your family.

The primary manifestation of Godliness in your life will be living a life characterized by My love. If you will learn to let everything you do and say be seasoned with love, then you are taking giant leaps toward helping My plan for your family to be manifest. This is not always easy, but the reward is worth the effort it takes. If you will allow the Spirit to work in you, then He will help you change anything in your life that does not look, act, or sound like My love.

My child, so far everything I have shared with you has dealt with outward manifestations of your relationship with Me. It is equally important that you learn to hold your family and the issues they face up before Me in prayer. I can and will intervene on their behalf, but you must be the one to release My ability in their lives through prayer. Pray that each of them take their proper place both in relationship with Me and as part of your family unit. Pray protection, healing, prosperity, and deliverance into their lives.

Point your finger at the devil and exercise the authority that I have given you over him on behalf of your family. He has no right to touch anything that is connected with you. When they need healing, lay your hands on them and believe Me to make them well. Pray that they be made prosperous and that they be delivered from the things that have been holding them in bondage. For further instruction, refer to Letter #23 on prayer to learn how to pray according to My will for them. As you lead by Godly example and release My ability into their lives through prayer, we will win them over, one at a time, to My plan.

My child, you are empowered to prosper in everything you put your hand to, so put your hand to being who you are called to be within your family and in praying for them to become who they are supposed to be. My plan is that your life and family be like Heaven on earth. I love you, and I am with you always to guide you and strengthen you. The verses that follow this letter are your starting point. Meditate on them and allow My Spirit to create an image of your family as you desire for them to be. Grab hold of that image by faith, and allow it to encourage you as you pray and believe for them to become everything that I have destined them to be. I love you.

Love,

Dad

Words from the Father's Heart

Acts 16:31—"They replied, 'Believe in the Lord Jesus, and you will be saved—you and your household.'"

Joshua 24:15—"But if serving the LORD (Daddy) seems undesirable to you, then choose for yourselves this day whom you will serve, whether the gods your forefathers served beyond the River, or the gods of the Amorites, in whose land you are living. But as for me and my household, we will serve the LORD (Daddy)."

Matthew 18:19-20—"Again, I tell you that if two of you on earth agree about anything you ask for, it will be done for you by my Father (Daddy) in heaven. For where two or three come together in my name, there am I with them."

Colossians 3:12-14—"Therefore, as God's (Daddy's) chosen people, holy and dearly loved, clothe yourselves with compassion, kindness, humility, gentleness and patience. Bear with each other and forgive whatever grievances you may have against one another. Forgive as the Lord forgave you.

And over all these virtues put on love, which binds them all together in perfect unity."

Ephesians 4:1-3—"As a prisoner for the Lord, then, I urge you to live a life worthy of the calling you have received. Be completely humble and gentle; be patient, bearing with one another in love. Make every effort to keep the unity of the Spirit through the bond of peace."

Questions from the Father's Heart

1) Identify and write down your roles in your family.______

____

____

____

____

____

____

2) What are your obligations as a Godly person to fulfill your roles? Be specific.______________________________

____

____

____

____

3) What areas can you think of that you need My help in being more Christ-like? ___________________________

____

____

____

____

____

4) What is your action plan to begin praying for your family and walking in love toward them as you should in order to fulfill your role in Godliness? Ask the Holy Spirit to help you; then be specific in laying out your plan.__________

____

____

____

____

Prayer to the Father

Daddy,

Thank You so much for the gift of my family. I recognize and understand that You gave them to me as part of Your perfect plan for my life. Please help me to begin to be the ______________________________ (fill in your role(s) here) that You have called me to be. Forgive me for the areas that I have not been the Christ-like person that I should be. Please help me shine like a light to my family, and please use me to help bring all of them into Your plan for their lives. Help me to be diligent to pray for them, and help me to always walk in love towards each of them regardless of what they do or say. I love You, and I know that I can walk in Your plan as You help me. In Jesus' name I pray.

Love,

____

Identifying with My Father

I yield to the Holy Spirit as He leads and guides me, and I live by the principles of my Heavenly Daddy's Word.

(Now, add your own thoughts.)

Letter #8:

Being a Godly Husband

My Dearest Son ______________________________,

(your name here)

I am so proud of you because you are My child. I have watched you grow from a child into a strong, Godly man, and I am pleased to call you My son. Son, I love you, and today I am going to teach you how to be a Christ-like husband, because there is a great weight of responsibility on your shoulders regarding your wife and your marriage. After reading this letter you will have greater understanding of your responsibility to your wife, and you will have a better foundation to go to My Word and get My wisdom for being a Christ-like husband. Please sit with Me, your Daddy, and let Me teach you how to honor Me by honoring the wife that I have given to you.

In order to learn your responsibilities as a husband, you must first understand your priorities as a Godly man. Son, your first priority is your relationship with Me. Your wife is your second priority, followed by your children third. Your fourth priority is the ministry that I have called you to do, and finally your job is your last priority. I have laid these priorities out clearly in My Word as the order your life is to follow. Now that you have a clear picture of My order, I can teach you to build a successful marriage on this foundation.

The earthly relationship of husband and wife is a symbol of the spiritual relationship between Jesus and the Church. My Word says that husbands should love their wives as Jesus loves the Church. Son, Jesus is the Master Husband after whom I desire to pattern all husbands. It was My perfect love inside of Jesus that enabled Him to love His Church enough to sacrifice Himself for it. He is your example of My love in the flesh, and by My Spirit I am transforming you into His image.

My son, I know you are asking, "How do I love my wife like Christ loves the Church?" You have such a pure heart. The answer can be found in My Word! First Corinthians 13:4-8 is My definition of love. In order to walk in Christ-like love for your wife, you must begin to apply My definition of love to your relationship with her. My love is patient and kind. It does not seek its own way or gain, and it always believes the best about others. My love does not change based on how I "feel" or based on circumstances. My perfect love is a fruit of the Spirit, and can only be cultivated by allowing Him to do His work in your heart.

If you will allow Him to work, the Spirit will begin to instruct you in the ways of love. Specifically, He will tell you what to say and how to act towards your wife. He will also tell you what not to say and how not to act towards your wife, if you are willing to follow His leading. As you become more sensitive to Him and yield to Him, He will transform you into the image of Jesus. As you are formed into Jesus' image, you will in turn be empowered to love your dear wife in the same way that Jesus loves His Church.

My Word says that you should dwell, or live, with your wife with understanding. Your wife thinks much differently than you do. As a Christ-like husband, you must nurture her, be understanding and patient with her, and strive to understand how she feels and thinks. I have created the two of you to have different perspectives so that through mutual respect and tolerance you will share a much more colorful and multifaceted life.

Son, you may never be called upon to give your life for your wife the way Jesus gave His life for His Church, but giving yourself does not necessarily mean dying physically. Giving yourself means growing to maturity in Christ and being a responsible, Godly man at all times. You are the spiritual authority in your house. You are responsible to provide the spiritual shelter for yourself and your household through your obedient relationship with Me.

It is your obligation to pray protection over your family and believe Me to keep them from all harm. It is your duty to learn how to believe My Word so that I can provide for you and your family through your faith. You must shepherd your wife, pray with her and for her, and guide her spiritually into a deeper relationship with Me. It is up to you to give yourself for her by walking in love toward her at all times, whether she walks in love or not. Son, this is a great responsibility on you, and I do not expect you to do it alone. I have placed My Spirit inside you to empower you to be a Christ-like husband.

Son, if you do not become all that you are called to be in Me, then there is no way your wife can become all that she is called to be in Me, either. As a result, you will be unable to become what I have called you to be as a couple. I have given your wife to you as a helper and a companion. I saw that you were alone, and I gave her to you to keep you company on the journey of life. I have a work for you to do that is beyond anything that you have ever imagined, and you cannot accomplish it without her help. In providing Christ-like love for her, you will create an atmosphere of stability in your home and in your relationship that will empower her to grow in strength and maturity in Christ. If she is secure in your love, then she can better support you in the work that I have laid out for you.

Love creates harmony like nothing else can. Dear son, the most important thing you can learn in life is that love is the answer to all things. When your race is finished, your course run, the most important accomplishment, next to your relationship with Me, is that you loved your wife like Christ loves you. I love you, My precious son. You are a strong, Godly man, and I am so proud of you!

Love,

Dad

WORDS FROM THE FATHER'S HEART

Genesis 2:18—"The LORD God (Daddy) said, 'It is not good for the man to be alone. I will make a helper suitable for him.'"

Ephesians 5:25-33—"Husbands, love your wives, just as Christ loved the church and gave himself up for her to make her holy, cleansing her by the washing with water through the word, and to present her to himself as a radiant church, without stain or wrinkle or any other blemish, but holy and blameless. In this same way, husbands ought to love their wives as their own bodies. He who loves his wife loves himself. After all, no one ever hated his own body, but he feeds and cares for it, just as Christ does the church—for we are members of his body. 'For this reason a man will leave his father and mother and be united to his wife, and the two will become one flesh.' This is a profound mystery—but I am talking about Christ and the church. However, each one of you also must love his wife as he loves himself, and the wife must respect her husband."

1 Peter 3:7—"Husbands, in the same way be considerate as you live with your wives, and treat them with respect as the weaker partner and as heirs with you of the gracious gift of life, so that nothing will hinder your prayers."

1 Corinthians 13:4-8—"Love is patient, love is kind. It does not envy, it does not boast, it is not proud. It is not rude, it is not self-seeking, it is not easily angered, it keeps no record of wrongs. Love does not delight in evil but rejoices with the truth. It always protects, always trusts, always hopes, always perseveres. Love never fails. . . ."

Ephesians 4:32—"Be kind and compassionate to one another, forgiving each other, just as in Christ God (Daddy) forgave you."

Questions from the Father's Heart

1) How has this letter opened your eyes to your role as a Godly husband? ____________

2) Identify some areas that you need to allow My Spirit to work in to form you into the image of Christ. ____________

3) What are some ways that you can begin to act more Christ-like today in your relationship with your wife? ____________

4) What will be your specific plan to allow My Spirit to have His way in you to form you into the husband that I desire for you to be? ____________

Prayer to the Father

Daddy,

Thank You so much for revealing to me Your plan for me as a husband. I realize that I have fallen short of being a truly Christ-like husband in many areas so please forgive me. Please form me more and more by Your Spirit into the image of Christ so that I can love my wife the way Jesus loves His Church. Help me always to speak and act towards her just like Jesus would, even if she does not respond in the same manner. I surrender to You, Daddy, so You can mold me into the vessel that You would have me to be. I love You. In Jesus' name I pray.

Love,

____

Identifying with My Father

I am being transformed daily into the image of Jesus so that I can love my wife like He does.

(Now, add your own thoughts.)

Letter #9: Being a Godly Father

My Dearest Son ______________________________,
(your name here)

I love you so very dearly. I delight greatly in you, and in the man you are becoming in Christ. The lessons of today's letter center around teaching you to be a Godly father. Please spend some time with Me today and allow Me to show you how to become a dad after your Heavenly Daddy's heart.

In the letter on being a Godly husband, I laid out your priorities for you as a Godly man with his Father's heart. According to My divine plan, your children are your third priority right behind your relationship with Me and your relationship with your wife. I have given you a tremendous responsibility both to mold your children like clay and to lead them in My righteous paths so that they are prepared to lead Godly lives of success when they leave your care.

My son, your children are My special gift to you. They are precious lives I have entrusted to your care to raise them to Godly maturity physically, mentally, and spiritually. My plan for you as a father is that you develop relationship and intimacy with Me, and in turn teach your children to walk in close relationship with Me. I know it can be scary at times to think of trying to raise children who will continue to honor Me with their lives and decisions when they are grown, but have no fear, My son! I am with you to teach and instruct you so that you can in turn do the same for your children.

My son, I know the questions of your heart: What does it truly mean to be a Godly father? How do I become a father after Your heart who honors You in the way I raise my children? Son, as always I am right here with the answers to your questions.

In many respects, being a Godly father is no different from being a Godly man. A Godly father is one who seeks to raise, teach, and guide his children in a way that pleases his Heavenly Father. A Godly man is a man who seeks My heart in all his ways. Do you see the connection, son? Being a Godly father is really just an extension of being a man with a heart after Me.

Son, the relationship that you share with your children is a reflection of your relationship with Me. Therefore, the best way for you to learn to raise your children in Godliness is to draw closer and closer to Me, your Heavenly Daddy. I am perfect love, and that perfect love enables Me to be a perfect Father. If you will first seek to strengthen your relationship with Me, you will be empowered by My Holy Spirit to be the kind of father to your children that I am to you. Son, read and meditate on the first letters concerning our relationship. As you apply the principles I have taught you to your everyday life, you will be on the path to making our relationship stronger. As our fellowship deepens, My Spirit will have more access to teach you to be a Christ-like example for your children to follow. As you embrace and get to know Me more, you will be transformed by My Spirit into My image—the image of your Heavenly Daddy.

Son, in addition to My spiritual wisdom and principles, you also need concrete, practical advice and wisdom on raising your children. First and foremost, you must learn to deal with your children in love at all times, regardless of the situation. Even though they are children, they always deserve love and respect. As the spiritual leader of your family, you must be a responsible, Christ-like example for your children to follow. Continually ask yourself the question, "What would my Heavenly Father have me do or say in this situation?"

My son, it is very important that you lead your children both in prayer and in Bible study, because if you do not teach your children My ways, no one else will. Also, do not ever discipline your children when you are angry, because this leads to ungodly actions and words that you will later regret. Anger does not produce the righteous life that I desire in either you or them, and they learn by your example. You must be loving and approachable even when they have done something wrong. Just as I promised you that I would always love and accept you no matter what, you too must learn to always accept your children in love even when they have done wrong. Allow them to have their own thoughts and opinions. Encourage them and make them feel as if their thoughts and feelings are valued. Pray for them always, in all things. I can intervene in their lives more readily if you will be diligent to pray for them.

Son, you must also be careful with your words, actions, and even your facial expressions, because your children will pick up on them and will imitate you. Children are extremely perceptive and very impressionable. You must remember that you are forming who they are, like clay, in everything you do. Go to the book of Proverbs and find My wisdom for raising your children. Continually ask for My wisdom to deal with them in every situation that you face, and I will be faithful to give it to you. Above all, My son, remember to act toward your kids according to My definition of love found in 1 Corinthians 13.

Son, you are My special kid, and I am very proud of you. In this letter I have given you some basic foundational truths that you can build upon to become the father that I desire you to be. As you learn to relate to Me as your Heavenly Father, and teach your children to do the same, they will be the blessing to you that I intend for them to be. I love you, son.

Love,

Dad

Words from the Father's Heart

Proverbs 22:6—"Train a child in the way he should go, and when he is old he will not turn from it."

Ephesians 6:4—"Fathers, do not exasperate your children; instead, bring them up in the training and instruction of the Lord."

Deuteronomy 6:4-9—"Love the LORD your God (Daddy) with all your heart and with all your soul and with all your strength. These commandments that I give you today are to be upon your hearts. Impress them on your children. Talk about them when you sit at home and when you walk along the road, when you lie down and when you get up. Tie them as symbols on your hands and bind them on your foreheads. Write them on the doorframes of your houses and on your gates."

Isaiah 54:13—"All your sons will be taught by the LORD (Daddy), and great will be your children's peace."

Proverbs 29:17—"Discipline your son, and he will give you peace; he will bring delight to your soul."

Questions from the Father's Heart

1) How has this letter opened your eyes to your responsibilities as a Godly father? ______________________

____

____

____

____

____

2) Write down all the responsibilities that you can think of that you have as a Godly father. ______________________

____

____

____

____

____

3) Identify and write down some ways that you have not been acting as a Christ-like father towards your children.

____

4) What can you do to begin to implement My definition of love into these areas and into your relationship with your children?

5) What is your plan to make sure that you care for your responsibilities as a father, according to My Word?

Prayer to the Father

Daddy,

Thank You so much for the wonderful children that You have given to me. I realize that I have many responsibilities as a Godly father. I know I have failed at times, and I ask You to forgive me. Please help me to be the father You would have me be. Please mold me into the image of Christ and His love so that I truly love and raise my children in the way that You would have me to. Please lead me, guide me, and direct me in the paths of a Godly father, and as You do I will do my best to be obedient. I love You. In Jesus' name I pray.

Love,

____

Identifying with My Father

As I am transformed into the image of Christ, I will be empowered to love my children as My Heavenly Daddy loves me. *(Now, add your own thoughts.)*

Letter #10:

Being a Godly Wife

My Dearest Daughter ______________________,

(your name here)

I am so proud of you because you are My child. I have watched you grow from a child into a strong, Godly woman, and I am pleased to call you My daughter. I love you, and today I am going to teach you how to be a Godly wife, because you have a big responsibility to your husband and to your marriage. After reading this letter, you will have a greater understanding of your responsibility to your husband, and you will have a better foundation for going to My Word to get My wisdom for being a Godly wife. Please sit with Me, your Daddy, and let Me teach you how to honor Me by honoring the husband I have given you.

In order to learn your responsibilities as a wife, you must first understand your priorities as a Godly woman. Your first priority is your relationship with Me. Your husband is your second priority, followed by your children third. Your fourth priority is helping your husband in the ministry that I have called him to do, and finally your job is your last priority. I have laid these priorities out clearly in My Word as to the order your life is to follow. Now that you have a clear picture of My order for your life, I can teach you to build a successful marriage on this foundation.

The earthly relationship of husband and wife is a symbol of the spiritual relationship between Jesus and the Church. My Word says that wives are to submit to their husbands as to the Lord Jesus. The Church and its relationship with Jesus is the model that I have set forth by which to pattern your life as a wife. It is the Church's loving submission to Jesus that allows Him to lead and guide her and His glory to be reflected in her. Similarly, as you step into greater submission both to Jesus as part of His Church and to your husband as unto the Lord, you will reflect the Godly image of marriage that I desire.

My child, I know you are asking, "How do I submit to my husband as unto the Lord?" You have such a pure heart. The first thing you need is to gain a greater understanding of My plan for the Church's surrender to the Lord Jesus, and then we can relate this to your relationship with your husband.

Jesus is the image of My perfect love, and He is My model of the perfect husband. His sacrifice transforms those who accept Him as Savior and Lord into His Heavenly bride. My child, you became born again by coming to an understanding of how much Jesus loves you, and then surrendering to and accepting Him because of His love. His love gave you the desire to accept Him, and as you grow and mature in Him, you will desire more and more to lay down your will for someone who loves you so dearly and wants only the best for you.

This loving relationship reflects My plan for the relationship between Jesus and His precious Church. Jesus' responsibility is to love the Church and give Himself for it. His death on the cross was a symbol of His love and His willingness to sacrifice Himself for His wife, the Church. The Church's response is to be in loving submission to its loving Lord. Similarly, your relationship with your husband is to be a reflection of the relationship between Christ and the Church.

As you grow in your love for Jesus and in submission to Him, you will gain greater revelation of how I desire your earthly marriage to work. I want to form your husband into the image of your Heavenly husband, Jesus, so that he loves you like Jesus loves you. This will be facilitated by you taking your place as a loving, submissive wife even when your husband does not act like Jesus. You are to reverence your husband and his final authority in your marriage just like you should honor Jesus as the Lord of your life. This means that you have to lay down your will and allow your husband to be the leader and the decision maker in the home. He is the head of the household. He is the final authority before Me. The only time you are not required to submit to him is if doing so will go against My Word and the commands of your Heavenly husband, Jesus.

My child, I know that this will not always be easy for you, but it is up to you to love your husband into the image of Christ. You will find My definition of love in 1 Corinthians 13:4-8. My love is patient and kind. It does not seek its own way or gain, and always believes the best about others. My love does not change based on how I "feel" or on circumstances. My perfect love is a fruit of the Spirit and can only be cultivated by allowing Him to do His work in your heart. If you will allow Him to work, the Spirit will begin to instruct you in the ways of love. Specifically, He will tell you what to say and how to act toward your husband. He will also tell you what not to say and how not to act toward your husband, if you will be willing to follow His leading.

As you become more sensitive to the Holy Spirit and yield to Him, He will transform you into the image of Jesus. As you are formed into Jesus' image, you will in turn be empowered to love your dear husband the way the Church is to love her Lord.

You must also hold him up before Me in prayer so that I can do My transforming work in his life. You are My gift to him and should always do your best to be the Godly wife in surrender to his authority. It is your Heavenly husband's desire that you submit to your earthly husband just as you submit to Him. Dearest child, the easiest way for you to do this is to pretend that your husband is Jesus. When you do this, you will begin to respond to him just as you would to your Savior and Lord.

My child, I do not expect you to be able to do this on your own. I have given you My precious Holy Spirit to live inside of you. He is the Spirit of your Lord and husband, Jesus. He will empower you to surrender to Jesus and to your husband as unto Jesus. Daughter, as you surrender to the Holy Spirit, you will find the power and freedom that come from walking in My plan for your life.

My child, if you do not become all that you are called to be in Me, then there is no way that your husband can become all that he is called to be in Me either. As a result, you will not become what I have called you to be as a couple. I have given you to your husband to be his helper and companion. I saw that you were alone, and I gave him to you to keep you company on the journey of life. I have a work for both of you to do that is beyond anything you have ever imagined, and you cannot accomplish it without each other's help.

In surrendering to him as unto the Lord, you will help create an atmosphere of stability in your home and in your relationship that will empower your husband to grow in strength and maturity in Christ. If he is secure in your love, then he can better accomplish the purposes that I have laid out for him. Love creates harmony like nothing else can.

Dearest princess, the most important thing you can learn in life is that love is the answer to all things. When your race is finished, your course run, the most important accomplishment you can have next to your relationship with Me is that you loved your husband like Christ loves you. I love you, My precious daughter. You are a strong, Godly woman and I am so proud of you!

Love,

Dad

WORDS FROM THE FATHER'S HEART

Proverbs 31:10-31—"A wife of noble character who can find? She is worth far more than rubies. Her husband has full confidence in her and lacks nothing of value. She brings him good, not harm, all the days of her life. She selects wool and flax and works with eager hands. She is like the merchant ships, bringing her food from afar. She gets up while it is still dark; she provides food for her family and portions for her servant girls. She considers a field and buys it; out of her earnings she plants a vineyard. She sets about her work vigorously; her arms are strong for her tasks. She sees that her trading is profitable, and her lamp does not go out at night. In her hand she holds the distaff and grasps the spindle with her fingers. She opens her arms to the poor and extends her hands to the needy. When it snows, she has no fear for her household; for all of them are clothed in scarlet. She makes coverings for her bed; she is clothed in fine linen and purple. Her husband is respected at the city gate, where he takes his seat among the elders of the land. She makes linen garments and sells them, and supplies the merchants with sashes. She is clothed with strength and dignity; she can laugh at the days to come. She speaks with wisdom, and faithful instruction is on her tongue. She watches over the affairs of her household and does not eat the bread of idleness. Her children arise and call her blessed; her husband also, and he praises her: 'Many women do noble things, but you surpass them all.' Charm is deceptive, and beauty is fleeting; but a woman who fears the LORD (Daddy) is to be praised. Give her the reward she has earned, and let her works bring her praise at the city gate."

Ephesians 5:22-24—"Wives, submit to your husbands as to the Lord. For the husband is the head of the wife as Christ is the head of the church, his body, of which he is the Savior. Now as the church submits to Christ, so also wives should submit to their husbands in everything."

1 Peter 3:1-2- "Wives, in the same way be submissive to your husbands so that, if any of them do not believe the word, they may be won over without words by the behavior of their wives, when they see the purity and reverence of your lives."

Genesis 2:18—"The LORD God (Daddy) said, 'It is not good for the man to be alone. I will make a helper suitable for him.'"

1 Corinthians 13:4-8—"Love is patient, love is kind. It does not envy, it does not boast, it is not proud. It is not rude, it is not self-seeking, it is not easily angered, it keeps no record of wrongs. Love does not delight in evil but rejoices with the truth. It always protects, always trusts, always hopes, always perseveres. Love never fails. . . ."

Ephesians 4:32—"Be kind and compassionate to one another, forgiving each other, just as in Christ God (Daddy) forgave you."

Questions from the Father's Heart

1) How has this letter opened your eyes to your role as a Godly wife? ______________________________

____

____

____

____

2) Identify some areas where you need to allow Me to work to form you into the image of Christ. ______________________________

____

____

____

____

3) What are some ways that you can begin to act more Christ-like today in your relationship with your husband?

____

____

____

____

____

4) What will be your specific plan to allow My Spirit to have His way in you to form you into the wife that I desire you to be?______________________________________

____

____

____

____

Prayer to the Father

Daddy,

Thank You so much for revealing to me Your plan for me as a wife. I realize that I have fallen short of being a truly Godly wife in many areas so please forgive me. Please form me into a more Godly woman so I can love and submit to my husband the way that You desire for the Church to submit to Jesus. Help me always to speak and act toward him just like Jesus would, even when he does not do the same. I surrender to You, Daddy, so You can mold me into the vessel that You would have me to be. I love You. In Jesus' name I pray.

Love,

____

Identifying with My Father

Just as I am growing in my love for my Lord Jesus,
I am maturing in my love for my husband.

(Now, add your own thoughts.)

Letter #11:

Being a Godly Mother

My Dearest Daughter ______________________,

(your name here)

I love you so very dearly. I delight greatly in you, and in the woman you are becoming in Christ. The lessons of today's letter center around teaching you to be a Godly mother. Please spend some time with Me today and allow Me to show you how to become a mom after your Heavenly Daddy's heart.

In the letter on being a Godly wife, I laid out your priorities for you as a Godly woman with her Father's heart. According to My divine plan, your children are your third priority right behind your relationship with Me and your relationship with your husband. I have given you a tremendous responsibility both to mold your children like clay and to lead them in My righteous paths so that they are prepared to lead Godly lives of success when they leave your care.

My child, your children are My special gift to you. They are precious lives I have entrusted to your care to raise to Godly maturity physically, mentally, and spiritually. My plan for you as a mother is that you develop relationship and intimacy with Me, and in turn teach your children to walk in close relationship with Me. I know it can be scary at times to think of trying to raise children who will continue to honor Me with their lives and decisions when they are grown, but have no fear, My child! I am with you to teach and instruct you so that you can in turn do the same for your children.

My child, I know the questions of your heart: What does it truly mean to be a Godly mother? How do I become a mother after Your heart who honors You in the way I raise my children? Princess, as always I am right here with the answers to your questions.

In many respects, being a Godly mother is no different from being a Godly woman. A Godly mother is one who seeks to raise, teach, and guide her children in a way that pleases her Heavenly Father. A Godly woman is a person who seeks My heart in all her ways. Do you see the connection, My child? Being a Godly mother is really just an extension of being a woman with a heart after Me.

My child, the relationship that you share with your children is a reflection of your relationship with Me. Therefore, the best way for you to learn to raise your children in Godliness is to draw closer and closer to Me, your Heavenly Daddy. I am perfect love, and that perfect love enables Me to be a perfect parent. If you will first seek to strengthen your relationship with Me, you will be empowered by My Holy Spirit to be the parent to your children that I am to you.

My child, read and meditate on the letters concerning our relationship. Begin to apply what I teach you there to your everyday life, and you will be on the path to making our relationship stronger. As our fellowship deepens, My Spirit will have more access to teach you to be a Christ-like example for your children to follow. As you embrace and get to know Me, you will be transformed by My Spirit into the image of your Heavenly Father.

My child, I know that in addition to My spiritual wisdom and principles, you also need concrete, practical advice and wisdom on raising your children. First and foremost, you must learn to deal with your children in love at all times, regardless of the situation. Even though they are children, they always deserve love and respect. As their spiritual leader next to your husband, you must be a responsible, Christ-like example for your children to follow. Continually ask yourself the question, "What would my Heavenly Father have me do or say in this situation?"

My child, it is very important that you and your husband lead your children both in prayer and in Bible study, because if you do not teach your children My ways, no one else will. Also, do not ever discipline your children when you are angry, because this leads to ungodly actions and words that you will later regret. Anger does not produce the righteous life that I desire in either you or them, and they learn by your example. You must be loving and approachable even when they have done something wrong. Just as I promised you that I would always love and accept you no matter what, you too must learn to always accept your children in love even when they have done wrong. Allow them to have their own thoughts and opinions. Encourage them and make them feel that their thoughts and feelings are valued. Pray for them always in all things. I can intervene in their lives more readily if you will petition Me on their behalf.

My child, you must also be careful with your words, actions, and even your facial expressions, because your children will pick up on them and will imitate you. Children are extremely perceptive, and very impressionable. You must remember that you are forming who they are, like clay, in everything you do. Go to the book of Proverbs and find My wisdom for raising your children. Continually ask for My wisdom to deal with them in every situation that you face, and I will be faithful to give it to you. Above all, My child, remember to act toward your children according to My definition of love found in 1 Corinthians 13.

Princess, you are My special child, and I am very proud of you. In this letter I have given you some basic foundational truths that you can build upon to become the mother that I desire you to be. As you learn to relate to Me as your Heavenly Father and teach your children to do the same, they will be the blessing to you that I intend for them to be. I love you!

Love,

Dad

Words from the Father's Heart

Proverbs 22:6—"Train a child in the way he should go, and when he is old he will not turn from it."

Deuteronomy 6:5-9—"Love the LORD your God (Daddy) with all your heart and with all your soul and with all your strength. These commandments that I give you today are to be upon your hearts. Impress them on your children. Talk about them when you sit at home and when you walk along the road, when you lie down and when you get up. Tie them as symbols on your hands and bind them on your foreheads. Write them on the doorframes of your houses and on your gates.

Isaiah 54:13—"All your sons will be taught by the LORD (Daddy), and great will be your children's peace."

Proverbs 29:17—"Discipline your son, and he will give you peace; he will bring delight to your soul."

Questions from the Father's Heart

1) How has this letter opened your eyes to your responsibilities as a Godly mother? ______________________________

____

____

____

____

2) Write down all the responsibilities that you can think of that you have as a Godly mother. ______________________

____

____

____

____

3) Identify and write down some ways that you have not been acting as a Godly mother towards your children.

____

____

____

____

____

4) What can you do to begin to implement My definition of love into these areas and into your relationship with your children? ______________________________

____

____

____

____

5) What is your plan to make sure that you care for your responsibilities as a mother, according to My Word? _____

____

____

____

____

Prayer to the Father

Daddy,

Thank You so much for the wonderful children that You have given to me. I realize that I have many responsibilities as a Godly mother. I know that at times I have failed, and I ask You to forgive me. Please help me to be the mother that You would have me to be. Please mold me into the image of Christ and His love so that I truly do love and raise my children in the way that You would have me to. Please lead me, guide me, and direct me in the paths of a Godly mother, and as You do, I will do my best to be obedient. I love You! In Jesus' name I pray.

Love,

____

Identifying with My Father

I am being molded by My Heavenly Daddy's love to become the mother that He would have me to be.

(Now, add your own thoughts.)

Letter #12:

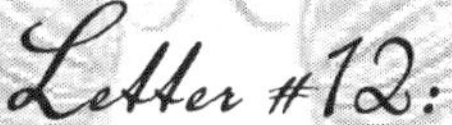

Praying for Your Family

My Child ________________________________,

(your name here)

I love you very much. Today I am going to teach you about praying for your family. In Letter #7, I taught you the importance of your family and My plan for it. I have emphasized the importance of praying for them time and time again, but in this letter I want to give you some specific guidance about lifting them up to Me.

I have given your family to you as a special gift. According to My perfect plan, there is no bond of love stronger than family. I have made the family to be a place of strength and refuge. Only through your prayers can you and your family begin to step into the wonderful plan that I have laid out for you.

My child, praying for your family can be difficult at times and is a task that requires both diligence and dedication. It is vital that you make a decision that you are going to be faithful to lift your family up according to My Word no matter what. Once you do, you will be prepared to stand in prayer for them until My Kingdom manifests in their lives.

My child, before I begin to teach you how to pray for your loved ones, there is a very important Kingdom principle that you must understand concerning the words of your mouth. According to My Word, your tongue holds the power of life and death. My Word also says, referring to your mouth, that as a fountain cannot flow with both bitter water and sweet, neither should My child's words be used to curse others. In fact, no unwholesome talk should come out of your mouth, but only what is helpful for building others up according to their needs. I define "unwholesome talk" as anything spoken that is out of line with My written Word. You must understand that not only are your prayers powerful, but every word that you speak is powerful, as well. If you pray for your loved ones in line with My Word, and then speak contrary to My Word concerning them, you are like a fountain with a flow of bitter water and sweet.

You cannot control your tongue in your own strength, so you must allow My Holy Spirit to bridle it and bring it in line with My Word. When you do, you will be planting seeds with your prayers for your family and watering them with My Word so that they bring forth a harvest, rather than planting My Word with your prayers and then uprooting the seeds with your words.

My child, your prayers for your family are effective. I hear each and every one of them. In order to pray effectively for your family, both saved and unsaved, every prayer for them must begin with a basis in My Word. Each member of your family, yourself included, needs My divine wisdom and guidance for their lives. They need My protection, prosperity, and health flowing in their lives. Refer to the letters I have written to you concerning these topics and begin to pray accordingly for your family.

You should also pray that My Spirit brings growth and maturity to the lives of your born-again family members. They need a greater manifestation of My Spirit's fruit in their lives, and this will come through a deeper relationship with Me. Trust Me to draw them into a closer fellowship with Me than they have ever experienced. I will be faithful to hear and act on your petitions.

My child, I hear the cries of your heart for those loved ones who are unsaved. I also know the pain of having lost loved ones all too well. I remember when you were lost and how My heart cried for you to come to Me and let Me be your Daddy. I will be faithful to My Word to bring your lost loved ones into My Kingdom, but you too must be faithful to stand on My Word to empower Me to work on their behalf. You must also understand that you are not striving against flesh and blood; you are striving against the powers of darkness that seek to control them and their actions.

You must use the authority that I have given you to deal with the forces of darkness, which are motivating your unsaved family members to live and act ungodly. The weapons of your warfare are not fleshly; they are spiritual. Please go to My letter about your authority and apply those principles to dealing with the forces of darkness on behalf of your lost loved ones. Couple what you learn there with the letter that teaches you how to deal with the devil, and you will be equipped to overcome the enemy who is at work in their lives. My child, you must continue to pray and believe Me for their salvation until it manifests. Be diligent to pray for them daily. Pray protection over them, and pray for the Holy Spirit to have His way in their hearts and minds.

My child, I cannot stress enough the importance of your prayers for your family. I have placed you as a bridge between your family and My power and ability to accomplish everything they need in their lives. Search My Word and find promises pertaining to every area of life and pray them over your family. Be diligent to pray for each of them daily. Let the Holy Spirit put a guard over your mouth so that you don't pull up any of the seed of My Word that you have sown with your prayers. As you are diligent, I will be faithful to perform My Word on behalf of your family. I love you, My faithful child.

Love,

Dad

Words from the Father's Heart

Proverbs 18:21—"The tongue has the power of life and death, and those who love it will eat its fruit."

James 3:9-12—"With the tongue we praise our Lord and Father (Daddy), and with it we curse men, who have been made in God's (Daddy's) likeness. Out of the same mouth come praise and cursing. My brothers, this should not be. Can both fresh water and salt water flow from the same spring? My brothers, can a fig tree bear olives, or a grapevine bear figs? Neither can a salt spring produce fresh water.

Ephesians 4:29—"Do not let any unwholesome talk come out of your mouths, but only what is helpful for building others up according to their needs, that it may benefit those who listen."

James 5:16b—"The prayer of a righteous man is powerful and effective."

Acts 16:31—"They replied, 'Believe in the Lord Jesus, and you will be saved—you and your household.'"

Psalm 19:14—"May the words of my mouth and the meditation of my heart be pleasing in your sight, O LORD (Daddy), my Rock and my Redeemer."

Questions from the Father's Heart

1) List your family members, along with some specific needs that they have, so you can begin to pray for them concerning those things. ____________________

____

____

____

____

2) Thinking back over some of the things you may have said, what could you speak instead concerning your family?

____

____

____

____

3) How can you begin to line all your words up with My Word concerning your family? (Hint: Allow the Holy Spirit to guard your mouth.) ______________________________

____

____

____

____

4) What is your plan to be diligent to pray and believe Me on behalf of your family so that My glory can manifest in their lives? ______________________________

____

____

____

____

Prayer to the Father

Daddy,

I recognize the importance of praying for my family and speaking right words over them at all times. I ask Your forgiveness for not praying for them enough, and for failing to speak Your Word over them, instead of what I see or feel. Please set a seal of the Holy Spirit over my mouth so that I speak only words that are pleasing in Your sight concerning my family. Help me to be diligent to pray for them according to Your Word. Please quicken my heart to pray for those closest to me at all times. I believe that as You help me to be diligent to pray and believe for them that You will manifest

Yourself in their lives in a real and powerful way. I love You! In Jesus' name I pray.

Love,

____

Identifying with My Father

My prayers for family members, based upon the promises from My Heavenly Daddy's Word, are powerful and effective. *(Now, add your own thoughts.)*

Letter #13:

Forgiving Others

My Dearest Child ___________________________,
(your name here)

Today we are going to make a transition from focusing on your relationship with your family to your relationships with others outside your family circle. This first letter in this new section teaches the principles of forgiveness toward those who have wronged you. Forgiveness flowing freely from a heart of love brings restoration and reveals My heart to the world. Unforgiveness, on the other hand, is a wicked tool the enemy uses to block My blessing and ability in the lives of believers. He uses it like a spiritual cancer to bring destruction to every life it touches. Together we will uncover his devices with the truth and learn to walk in forgiveness and love.

My dearest child, I know there have been times people have hurt you or given you cause to take up offense. It breaks My heart to see pain come into your life. Unfortunately, because you live in a fallen world, at times you will be faced with situations that require you to make a choice between forgiveness, which brings healing and unforgiveness which separates you from My ability to work in your life.

What makes forgiveness so important in the life of a believer? To answer this question let's take a look at the role that love and forgiveness played in the life of Jesus. As a man, He was a perfect image of My love manifest in the flesh. He died a horrible death to forgive all sin, and with His dying breath He forgave those who crucified Him. If you are to fulfill the destiny that I have laid out for you, then you must be molded into this image of Christ-like love. To accomplish this you must also learn to forgive others just as you have been forgiven, for Jesus' life illustrates that true love requires unconditional forgiveness.

What makes unforgiveness in a believer's life so dangerous? Unforgiveness removes you from the walk of love because you cannot truly love someone without forgiving them. My Word says that your faith works by love. This means that if you are carrying unforgiveness in your heart toward another, then your faith will not work properly. Faith connects you to Me and to My promises, so if your faith is not working properly then you are disconnected from the very things that give you life.

Remember, I am the Vine and you are a branch. Apart from Me you can do nothing. Now can you see how, like a pebble dropped in a pond, even a little unforgiveness has far-reaching effects? If you allow the seed of unforgiveness to take root in your heart and cultivate it, then it will ultimately produce a bitter harvest of destruction in your life.

Forgiveness toward the offender, on the other hand, works to bring blessing into your life because you are walking in love. Your faith can work unhindered, and My ability can flow more readily in your life. Sometimes choosing to forgive rather than be offended can be difficult. I do not expect you to be able to walk in forgiveness in your own strength. Your Friend and Comforter, the Holy Spirit, is with you to help you embrace forgiveness like Jesus did.

Here's a simple example that will help you to apply the principles of forgiveness taught in this letter. Let's pretend that your life is a nicely furnished room, and that someone has come in and thrown papers and trash all over the floor and made a real mess. Let's call this mess opportunities for offense and unforgiveness. Now, what are you going to do? Are you going to allow that mess to stay in your life or are you going to clean it up and get rid of it? In your imagination, take a box and pick up all the trash that they have strewn about in your room. Once you have picked up all the junk, let's close the box together. Now, let's take it out to the trash can and throw it away. It's gone!

Dearest child, do this in your imagination concerning any offenses and hurts you have been holding. Ask your Friend, the Holy Spirit, to help you pack up all those hurts and offenses and throw them away like trash. Declare in the name of Jesus that you forgive anyone who has hurt you. Please ask Me to heal your heart from the hurts, and I will be faithful to do that. When the memory of those offenses tries to come back, remember what I have taught you today and act accordingly. I am confident that you will not allow unforgiveness back in your life because with the Holy Spirit's help, you have packed it up and thrown it all away. My child, as you act on what I have taught you, you will begin to walk in freedom from all the hurts of the past. I desire to see you free in every area of your life because I love you.

Love,

Dad

Words from the Father's Heart

Colossians 3:13—"Bear with each other and forgive whatever grievances you may have against one another. Forgive as the Lord forgave you."

Matthew 5:44-45—"But I tell you: Love your enemies and pray for those who persecute you, that you may be sons of your Father (Daddy) in heaven."

Mark 11:25—"And when you stand praying, if you hold anything against anyone, forgive him, so that your Father (Daddy) in heaven may forgive you your sins."

Questions from the Father's Heart

1) Is there anyone who has wronged you that you have not forgiven? _________ On a separate sheet of paper, write down the hurts and wrongs done to you that you have had trouble forgiving.

2) Make the following confession over every one of the offenses: In the name of Jesus, I forgive (say the person's

name) for (say the offense). I choose to walk in forgiveness and love like Jesus did.

3) Now, tear up the paper and throw it in the trash like in the example I gave you in the letter. Write down your thoughts and feelings about the forgiveness you just embraced. ______________________________

____

____

____

____

4) Write down your plan of action to take next time an offense or a hurt comes your way so you can immediately forgive the offender and continue to walk in My blessing flow. ______________________________

____

____

____

____

PRAYER TO THE FATHER

Daddy,

In obedience to Your Word, I forgive anyone who has offended or hurt me in any way. Please help me to walk in love and forgiveness like Jesus did. I can't do this on my own. I need Your help. Please forgive me for carrying offenses towards others. From this point forward I will follow the example You gave me in this letter to walk in forgiveness. I love You. In Jesus' name I pray.

Love,

____

Identifying with My Father

I choose to walk in love and forgiveness just like my Heavenly Daddy. *(Now, add your own thoughts.)*

Letter #14:

Praying for Others

Dearest ________________________________,

(your name here)

Thank you so much for taking time to read this letter today. I greatly enjoy writing these letters that challenge you to greater growth in Me. You are growing strong in our relationship and in My Word, and I am so proud of you. Today I want to teach you about praying for other people.

Praying for others is something that is often overlooked by many of my children because their lives are so busy. I know it seems that there are so many things to do that you hardly have time to pray for yourself and those closest to you, let alone take time to apply your faith on behalf of others. My child, I want to reveal My heart to you regarding those around you.

Jesus said, "Greater love has no one than this, that he lay down his life for his friends" (John 15:13). Laying down your life does not necessarily mean dying on a cross like Jesus did. It's being willing to give of yourself for others. It can be as simple as stopping to say a quick prayer for someone you know is in need. Jesus specifically mentioned "friends" in the above verse, but who are your friends? Jesus answered this question with the parable of "The Good Samaritan."

In Luke 10, a lawyer testing Jesus asks Him who qualifies as his "neighbor" from the Old Testament passage, "'Love the Lord your God with all your heart and with all your soul and with all your strength and with all your mind'; and, 'Love your neighbor as yourself'" (Luke 10:27). Jesus' reply is known as the parable of the Good Samaritan.

When Jesus told this parable, there was a history of racial hatred between the Jews and the Samaritans. They despised and would have nothing do with each other. The Jews particularly hated the Samaritans because they were not of pure Jewish blood and were considered unfit to fellowship with because they were "unclean" according to Jewish tradition. The narrative of the story relates how a traveling Jewish man was robbed, beaten, and left for dead by thieves. Various people from his own country passed and left him lying near death. Then a Samaritan man happened along the road and saw the Jewish traveler lying where he had been left by the thieves. Every one of the Jewish man's countrymen ignored his suffering, yet the Samaritan, though hated and outcast by the Jewish people, stopped, helped him, and cared for his every need. Through this story Jesus teaches us that for a child of God, everyone is a "neighbor."

The same principle applies to laying down your life for your "friends" and "neighbors" as Jesus taught. Laying down your life in prayer for others is one of the best possible uses of your time. It seems that everyone thinks that the person on stage preaching My Word to thousands is something great in My Kingdom, but that man or woman is no more anointed than you are. Everyone is called to walk a different path. You are a success, if you are where I have placed you. Everyone is called to pray for others.

For example, when you see a need on TV, stop and pray a quick prayer for those people who need My help. You don't have to pray for an hour. It only takes a moment to release My ability into others' lives. Be quick to pray for others: family, friends, coworkers, etc. People need My intervention in their lives, and your prayer of faith brings Me on the scene. You have the ability to release My power into the lives of your "friends" and "neighbors."

Ask My Holy Spirit to give you a burden to pray for others, and to prompt you to pray for those in need with a heart of compassion. He will certainly do that, because it is My will to be involved in everyone's life. As you do this, you will be sowing seed that will bring forth a blessed harvest. If you will pray for others, then you will have others praying for you when you need it, and I will also be able to bless you more richly. Look at the life of Job. He went through so many trials and tribulations, but I was able to restore him when he prayed for his friends. My child, you are righteous and your prayers are powerful. Begin to release My ability today on behalf of others. I love you, and I will lead you in My paths of righteousness.

Love,

Dad

Words from the Father's Heart

John 15:13—"Greater love has no one than this, that he lay down his life for his friends."

Deuteronomy 6:5—"Love the LORD your God (Daddy) with all your heart and with all your soul and with all your strength."

Leviticus 19:18b—"Love your neighbor as yourself."

James 5:16 NKJV—"Confess your trespasses to one another, and pray for one another, that you may be healed. The effective, fervent prayer of a righteous man avails much."

Matthew 5:43-44 NKJV—"You have heard that it was said, 'You shall love your neighbor and hate your enemy.' But I say to you, love your enemies, bless those who curse you, do good to those who hate you, and pray for those who spitefully use you and persecute you."

2 Corinthians 2:14-15 NKJV—"Now thanks be to God (Daddy) who always leads us in triumph in Christ, and through us diffuses the fragrance of His knowledge in every place. For we are to God (Daddy) the fragrance of Christ among those who are being saved and among those who are perishing."

Job 42:10—"And the Lord (Daddy) restored Job's losses when he prayed for his friends. Indeed the Lord (Daddy) gave Job twice as much as he had before."

Questions from the Father's Heart

1) Can you think of times where you have felt led to pray for someone and did not because you were in a hurry or felt you did not have the time?__________________________

2) Identify and write down the names of some people you can begin to pray for on a regular basis for whom you have not prayed for before. _________________________

3) How can you begin to be more aware of the needs of others and lift those up to Me in prayer? ______________

Prayer to the Father

Daddy,

Thank You so much for revealing to me the importance of praying for others. I ask Your forgiveness for the times that I have been too busy and have failed to make the most of an opportunity to pray for someone else. As You help me, I will begin to be more diligent to lay down my life in prayer for those around me. Please help me to be aware of others' needs and pray for them with compassion. I love You. In Jesus' name I pray.

Love,

____

Identifying with My Father

I am following Jesus' example to lay down my life for others just like He laid down his life for me.

(Now, add your own thoughts.)

Letter #15: Representing Christ to the World

Dearest Heart _______________________________,

(your name here)

I chose you before you were born, and I am so glad that you are My own special child. I love you so much, and I am always with you no matter where you go. I enjoy spending time with you, and today I want to teach you about sharing your faith by representing Christ to the world. My child, at this moment countless souls all over the world are lost and dying because they do not know Jesus as their Savior and Lord. Each and every one of these lives is infinitely precious to Me, and I am intent on seeing them enter My Kingdom as My children. As a loving Father, I have provided the way for them to enter fellowship with Me through My Son, Jesus; however, the work of harvesting the souls belongs to My children who are empowered by My Holy Spirit.

Before ascending to Heaven, Jesus commissioned His disciples to go into all the world and preach the good news to everyone through the power of the Holy Spirit. My child, this commission was not only for the first disciples, but also for every person who accepts Jesus as Savior. When you received Christ, you became a royal ambassador of My Kingdom to the world.

In order to effectively reflect Jesus to the world, you must be transformed into His image. This transformation process is the destiny of every one of My children as they yield to the work of the Spirit in their lives. My Word teaches that in Christ the veil of sin is removed from your heart, enabling you to understand spiritual things. My Word is a spiritual mirror, and gazing into it reflects who you are in My Kingdom. If you embrace this image and surrender to My Spirit, then He will transform you into what you see in My Word. Jesus and the Word are one and the same, so if you are transformed into the image of the Word, then you are being transformed into the image of the Lord Jesus. You cannot accomplish this on your own, so I have placed My Holy Spirit inside you to transform you into the image of your big brother, Jesus.

I know you are wondering how to represent Jesus to the world according to My plan. The first thing you should do is begin to pray for those who are lost. Your prayers will give greater entrance to the Holy Spirit to work in their lives. He will prepare the ground of their hearts for the seed of My Word to be sown, and will make opportunities for you witness to those whose hearts He has been preparing. Ask Him to help you be a Christ-like example with your life, and to give you the words they need to hear. He will gladly help you to be an example of Jesus' love and power to those around you, because your life speaks volumes about who's inside you before you ever speak a word. Always remember that if the fruit of your life does not reflect the words you speak, then your witness for Christ is damaged regardless of what you say.

My child, you must learn to be sensitive to the Holy Spirit as I have taught you in other letters because this will enable you to hear and respond quickly when He speaks to you. When He speaks, be obedient so that He can bless others by your obedience. Finally, plant the seed of My Word abundantly in your heart, because doing so will give the Holy Spirit more to work with when using you to minister to others. By My Spirit you will reflect My love and character to the world. I love you so much, My child!

Love,

Dad

Words from the Father's Heart

2 Corinthians 5:20-21—"We are therefore Christ's ambassadors, as though God (Daddy) were making his appeal through us. We implore you on Christ's behalf: Be reconciled to God (Daddy). God (Daddy) made him who had no sin to be sin for us, so that in him we might become the righteousness of God (Daddy)."

Matthew 5:14-16—"You are the light of the world. A city on a hill cannot be hidden. Neither do people light a lamp and put it under a bowl. Instead they put it on its stand, and it gives light to everyone in the house. In the same way, let your light shine before men, that they may see your good deeds and praise your Father (Daddy) in heaven."

Matthew 10:19-20—"But when they arrest you, do not worry about what to say or how to say it. At that time you will be given what to say, for it will not be you speaking, but the Spirit of your Father (Daddy) speaking through you."

2 Corinthians 3:17-18—"Now the Lord is the Spirit, and where the Spirit of the Lord is, there is freedom. And we, who with unveiled faces all reflect the Lord's glory, are being transformed into his likeness with ever-increasing glory, which comes from the Lord, who is the Spirit."

Questions from the Father's Heart

1) Who can you think of in your life who needs to see Christ reflected in you?______________________________

2) What are some ways that you can think of to begin representing Him to them?______________________________

3) How will you begin to act on the ideas that you have written down?______________________________

Prayer to the Father

Daddy,

Thank You so much for saving me, and working to mold me into the image of Christ. I know that Your plan is that I be a reflection of my Savior, Jesus, to the world. You have started a good work in me, and I know that You will be faithful to complete it. Please transform me into the image of Christ by the Holy Spirit so that I can truly represent Jesus to those around me. Help me to be Your light which shines into others' lives. I love you! In Jesus name I pray.

Love,

____

Identifying with My Father

The fruit of the Spirit in my life is reflected by the words that I speak and by my actions.

(Now, add your own thoughts.)

Letter #16:

Being a Godly Friend

Dear ______________________________________,

(your name here)

You are My beloved child, and you please Me greatly. I am so proud of your growth in Me and My Word. Today's letter will focus on teaching you how to be a Godly friend, and show forth Christ more richly in those relationships.

Your friends fall into one of two categories, saved and unsaved. While the principles of being a Godly friend do not change, the way you interact with each one will be dictated by their relationship with Me. It is always your responsibility to pray for your friends. Lift them up before Me, and intercede on their behalf so that My ability can flow into their lives because of your prayers. Be quick to listen to what they have to say and hold their words in confidence. When they open up to you and share their heart, it will give you greater understanding to pray more effectively for them.

My child, seek to strengthen your relationship with Me, because as you do, you will learn to walk in a greater realm of Christ's love, and you will be able to more fully reflect that love in your relationships with your friends.

When interacting with your friends who are born again, rejoice together with them as fellow believers. Spend time with them in prayer and in My Word. As iron sharpens iron, you will sharpen each other in Godliness. Become accountable to one another as brothers and sisters in Christ to encourage spiritual growth.

Remember that you are My representative in this world, and the only way your unsaved friends can see that they need Me is through the witness of your life. You must do everything you can to point them to Christ with your life so they will know that your relationship with Him is real, and as a result, they will come to desire Him for themselves.

I will finish this letter with a question for you to answer. Ask yourself, "What kind of friend do I want someone to be to me?" Now, go and be that friend to them! If you keep yourself in love, then you will never have to ask yourself if you are being a Godly friend. Look to My Spirit because He will enable you to minister My love to them and be a true friend like Jesus. Ask Him for His help, and He will gladly give it. I love you, My child.

Love,

Dad

Words from the Father's Heart

Proverbs 17:17—"A friend loves at all times, and a brother is born for adversity."

Proverbs 18:24—"A man of many companions may come to ruin, but there is a friend who sticks closer than a brother."

Proverbs 27:17—"As iron sharpens iron, so one man sharpens another."

John 15:13—"Greater love has no one than this, that he lay down his life for his friends."

Questions from the Father's Heart

1) Make a list of your friends and their specific needs. Begin to pray over them and their needs as I have taught you.

____

____

____

____

____

____

____

2) What specific action can you take toward each of them in order to reveal Christ to them in a greater way? Write down what you plan to do for each one. _______________

____

____

____

____

____

____

Prayer to the Father

Daddy,

I recognize that being a Godly friend is important because through friendship You can open doors to reveal and share Jesus that might not otherwise be open. Help me to draw closer to You so I can more fully reflect Christ and His love to my friends. Help me to be a Godly, Christ-like example to my friends who are saved and unsaved. Help me to be a friend like Jesus—one who sticks closer than a brother at all times. In Jesus' name I pray.

Love,

____

Identifying with My Father

As I grow in my relationship with my Heavenly Daddy, my friends will see the light of Jesus shine through my life.

(Now, add your own thoughts.)

Letter #17:

Being a Godly Employee

Dear ______________________________________,

(your name here)

I love you very much. As you grow in My love, understand that your relationship with Me should touch every area of your life, every relationship, every action, every word. Even your performance and attitudes as an employee should be governed by being My child.

Being a Godly employee is primarily characterized by being a Godly person. There are two basic areas where Christ in you must shine through in order for you to be the kind of employee I want you to be.

The first is showing forth Christ and His love in your workplace. Please refer back to the letter I wrote you about sharing your faith by representing Christ in your daily life. This letter will guide you into greater truth about how to reflect Christ more fully in every area of life including your workplace. As His love and heart shine through you, you will glorify Me and draw your coworkers to Me.

Second, you must perform your work in a Christ-like manner. Remember the old saying about your actions speaking louder than your words? Well, this is very true when it comes to your performance in the workplace. If you profess to be a Christian, but fail to maintain a solid work ethic, you will discount your witness with your actions. You are to be an example of what a model employee should be. This is not always easy, but remember that I said in My Word to do your work as though Jesus were your master.

My child, I am proud of you. Let me encourage you to pray for your coworkers and your management. Pray for the company that employs you. Bless your workplace and its environment, and do your best to be a blessing in it. Please don't get caught up in the workplace gossip and murmurings. Those things are ungodly and do not manifest My love. Remember that My Word says to do everything without complaining. Give thanks to Me in all things, and let My praise continually be on your lips. If you will let the fruit of your lips bring forth praise, and act as though Jesus were your boss, you will be a happier, more Godly employee.

Ask your Friend, the Holy Spirit, to identify any ways that you have not been the Godly employee that you should be. When He does, ask for forgiveness and His help to reflect Christ on your job. As you follow the leading of the Holy Spirit, you will grow into the Godly employee that I desire for you to be. I love you!

Love,

Dad

Words from the Father's Heart

Ephesians 6:5-8—"Slaves, obey your earthly masters with respect and fear, and with sincerity of heart, just as you would obey Christ. Obey them not only to win their favor when their eye is on you, but like slaves of Christ, doing the will of God (Daddy) from your heart. Serve wholeheartedly, as if you were serving the Lord, not men, because you know that the Lord will reward everyone for whatever good he does, whether he is slave or free."

Hebrews 13:15—"Through Jesus, therefore, let us continually offer to God (Daddy) a sacrifice of praise—the fruit of lips that confess his name."

Psalm 34:1—"I will extol the LORD (Daddy) at all times; his praise will always be on my lips."

Philippians 2:14-15—"Do everything without complaining or arguing, so that you may become blameless and pure, children of God (Daddy) without fault in a crooked and depraved generation, in which you shine like stars in the universe."

Questions from the Father's Heart

1) In what areas have you succeeded and in what areas have you failed in being a Godly employee?________________

____

____

____

____

____

2) With My Spirit's help, what is your plan to change those areas and begin being the person you are called to be in the workplace? ______________________________

____

____

____

____

PRAYER TO THE FATHER

Daddy,

Please forgive me for any areas that I have failed to reflect Christ in the workplace, both through my actions and my work ethic. As You help me, I will be a light for Christ to my coworkers. With Your help, I will begin to perform my work as though Jesus were my boss. I will also begin to pray for my company, my management, and my fellow employees. Please help me not to complain, gossip, or take part in any activity at work which does not please You. Please help me to be the kind of Godly employee that You would have me to be. In Jesus' name I pray.

Love,

____

Identifying with My Father

With the help of the Holy Spirit, Jesus' love shines through me, both in my words and in my performance on the job. *(Now, add your own thoughts.)*

Letter #18: Dealing with Difficult People

Dear ______________________________,

(your name here)

I love you so much, and My concern for you extends to even the smallest areas of your life. To show you how much I care about you, I am going to impart My wisdom to you today about dealing with difficult people to enable you to be successful even in difficult situations.

The truth is that difficult people will always be a part of life whether at work, at church, or even in your own family. Since these people will always be a part of life, learning to interact successfully with them will greatly multiply your peace and happiness. What are the key steps to successful interaction with these people? First, you must learn to apply Paul's words when he writes in 2 Corinthians to "regard no one from a worldly point of view." Whether saved or unsaved, I have a plan and a purpose for every person on earth. If a person is saved, then I am working in their heart to transform them into the image of Christ. If they are unsaved, then I am wooing them by My Spirit to accept My gift of salvation.

You must understand that I see everyone not as they are, but as living in the fullness of what I have for them; acting and talking and treating others like Christ. Once you begin seeing these people through My eyes, it will be easier for you to maintain Godliness in your interaction with them.

Second, you must decide that you are going to love difficult people. Respond to them in love even when they mistreat you, because you will not get anywhere reacting to those people in a fleshly manner. I know that sometimes your flesh would just like to tell someone off, but that would only further the problem and strengthen the enemy's position. In your interaction with them, try to treat them as you think Christ would treat them, because your choice to walk in love will begin opening the door for the Holy Spirit to work in their hearts. As you keep yourself in love, your faith can work more effectively on their behalf, and your heart will remain more peaceful, as well.

Third, you must begin to pray fervently for those difficult people. Their words and actions are motivated by the enemy. My Word says that your "struggle is not against flesh and blood, but against the rulers, against the authorities, against the powers of this dark world and against the spiritual forces of evil in the heavenly realms" (Ephesians 6:14).

Remember that your weapons are spiritual, and that "they have divine power to demolish strongholds" (2 Corinthians 10:4). You need to exercise your authority over the spirits of the enemy who are motivating those people to behave the way they do. Pray that My Spirit has His way in their lives and changes them from the inside out so they will learn to act in love.

Finally, you must refuse to allow the devil to manipulate anyone into getting you upset and frustrated, because when you do, it severs our fellowship and gets you out of the Spirit. This means that you need to try to limit your interaction with some people as much as possible while believing Me to change them. You'll find dealing with them is like trying to wade through a spiritual swamp. You constantly have to struggle to stay spiritually focused while their attitudes and actions are pulling you down. In other situations, you will have to interact with these people on a regular basis. In those cases, you must follow the plan I have laid out for you above, and ask for My help to keep you walking in the Spirit.

My child, bind the ability of the enemy to motivate anyone against you to try to get you out of the Spirit. This will help cut down on the difficult people and situations that cross your path. Ask the Holy Spirit to help you walk in love at all times and to deal successfully with difficult people. I love you, My child, and I am always here with you through the Sprit.

Love,

Dad

Words from the Father's Heart

2 Corinthians 5:14-16—"For Christ's love compels us, because we are convinced that one died for all, and therefore all died. And he died for all, that those who live should no longer live for themselves but for him who died for them and was raised again. So from now on we regard no one from a worldly point of view. Though we once regarded Christ in this way, we do so no longer."

Matthew 5:43-45a—"You have heard that it was said, 'Love your neighbor and hate your enemy.' But I tell you: Love your enemies and pray for those who persecute you, that you may be sons of your Father (Daddy) in heaven."

Ephesians 6:12—"For our struggle is not against flesh and blood, but against the rulers, against the authorities, against the powers of this dark world and against the spiritual forces of evil in the heavenly realms."

2 Corinthians 10:3-5—"For though we live in the world, we do not wage war as the world does. The weapons we fight with are not the weapons of the world. On the contrary, they have divine power to demolish strongholds. We demolish arguments and every pretension that sets itself up against the knowledge of God (Daddy), and we take captive every thought to make it obedient to Christ."

Questions from the Father's Heart

1) Identify the people in your life who can be difficult to deal with. What makes interacting with them hard at times?

____

____

____

____

____

____

2) How has this letter helped you to view these people differently than you did before? ______________________

____

____

____

____

____

3) What can you do to begin to believe Me to change these people so that they reflect Godliness in their words and actions? ______________________________________

____

____

____

4) What is your specific plan of action to successfully interact with these people, and stay in the Spirit even when they are not? ______________________________________

____

____

____

____

PRAYER TO THE FATHER

Daddy,

Thank You so much for revealing to me how to successfully deal with difficult people. Please forgive me for not always responding and interacting in love with the ones in my life who can be trying. Help me see them through Your eyes and to do as Your Word says, and "regard no one from a worldly point of view." Help me to avoid being drawn into conflict with them, and to always respond to everyone in love regardless of how they treat me. Help me to begin to pray for these people and believe You to change them so that their lives reflect Godly character and love. With Your help I will be a Christ-like example for these people. In Jesus' name I pray.

Love,

____

Identifying with My Father

With my Heavenly Daddy's help I will follow His plan to love and pray for even the most difficult people in my life, because He loves them just as much as He loves Jesus.

(Now, add your own thoughts.)

Dearest Child ______________________________,

(your name here)

You are the apple of My eye, and I rejoice in you greatly. I love you so much, and I am so excited to be writing this letter to you today. This first "Kingdom Principles" letter deals with salvation, My greatest gift to you, and will be foundational to your understanding each of the topics covered in the rest of this section. The doctrine of salvation is among the most basic laid out in the New Testament, and only by understanding it can you grow to maturity in Christ on a firm foundation. Please sit with Me and see My heart as I unfold to you the greatest story ever told.

The story of salvation did not begin 2000 years ago when My Son, Jesus, was crucified and raised from the dead. It is a story much older than the history of man. Salvation was wrought by the strength of My hand in the ageless past before the world was founded. I am Jehovah, and I knew the end from the very beginning. Even before I formed the world, I knew that sin would enter it, and that the only way I could rescue humanity from the grasp of the evil one was to send my Son, Jesus, to die as a perfect sacrifice for all sin.

My child, I am God, and My nature is perfect and pure. I created man in My image, with My nature, because I wanted special children to share in rich fellowship with and to love. Unfortunately, man sinned and was completely cut off from Me as a result. Even though I am love, My perfect nature will not allow Me to have any fellowship with sin. My heart's desire was to bring My precious ones back into fellowship with Me because humanity was lost and powerless to save itself.

In the court of the universe, the only way that sin can be paid for is with an innocent sacrifice. What could be done? Mankind was tainted by sin and powerless to bring a worthy sacrifice to satisfy the demands of justice. I had to make the sacrifice! Jesus, My Son, had to come to earth as perfect God in the form of man. He remained perfect until He was sacrificed on a cross and bore the judgment of sin for all mankind. I sacrificed My Son on the cross so that I could have you as My special child.

Dearest heart, if you had been the only person on earth who needed saving from sin, I would have sent Jesus to die just for you. Jesus would have died just for you so that you could become My special child. He died for the millions, but He also died for each one.

Entering into My salvation plan is simple.You must confess with your mouth the lordship of Jesus over your life, and believe in your heart that I raised Him from the dead. Once you have done this, you have received My free gift of salvation, and we are then in perfect unity and harmony.You are restored to right relationship with Me, and you can now stand in My presence as though sin had never entered your life.

My child, receiving salvation is the first step to walking in all the fullness that I have for you. Rejoice, My child, because your name is written in the Lamb's Book of Life, and you will spend eternity with Me. I love you! I love you! I love you!!!

Love,

Dad

Words from the Father's Heart

Romans 5:8-11,17—"But God (Daddy) demonstrates his own love for us in this: While we were still sinners, Christ died for us. Since we have now been justified by his blood, how much more shall we be saved from God's (Daddy's) wrath through him! For if, when we were God's (Daddy's) enemies, we were reconciled to him through the death of his Son, how much more, having been reconciled, shall we be saved through his life! Not only is this so, but we also rejoice in God (Daddy) through our Lord Jesus Christ, through whom we have now received reconciliation . . . For if, by the trespass of the one man, death reigned through that one man, how much more will those who receive God's (Daddy's) abundant provision of grace and of the gift of righteousness reign in life through the one man, Jesus Christ."

John 3:16-17—"For God (Daddy) so loved the world that he gave his one and only Son, that whoever believes in him shall not perish but have eternal life. For God (Daddy) did not send his Son into the world to condemn the world, but to save the world through him."

Ephesians 2:8-9—"For it is by grace you have been saved, through faith—and this not from yourselves, it is the gift of God (Daddy)—not by works, so that no one can boast."

Romans 10:6,8-10—"But the righteousness that is by faith says . . . 'The word is near you; it is in your mouth and in your heart,' that is, the word of faith we are proclaiming: That if you confess with your mouth, 'Jesus is Lord,' and believe in your heart that God (Daddy) raised him from the dead, you will be saved. For it is with your heart that you believe and are justified, and it is with your mouth that you confess and are saved."

Questions from the Father's Heart

1) Have you accepted My salvation plan by receiving Jesus as your Lord and Savior? _______ If not, what has kept you from doing so? ________________________________

____

____

____

____

2) How has this letter helped to make My plan of salvation clearer to you? ________________________________

____

____

____

3) Think for a few minutes and write down your thoughts about the importance of your salvation experience.

4) How has this experience changed your life? In what ways should it make a greater impact on your life?

Prayer to the Father

Daddy,

Thank You so much for your gift of salvation. Thank You, Jesus, for dying on the cross for me so that I could be saved. Please continue to reveal Your great love to me, and help me to grow and mature in Christ. I am so humbled that if I had been the only person on earth who needed a Savior that Jesus would have died just for me. Please help me to continue to live every day for Him. I rejoice that I have been made able to stand in Your presence completely free from the stain of sin. I love You! In Jesus' name I pray.

Love,

____

Identifying with My Father

I am my Heavenly Daddy's special child because Jesus loved me enough to give his life for me.

(Now, add your own thoughts.)

Prayer to Receive Salvation

Heavenly Father,

As I was reading this letter, I realized that I have never received Your free gift of salvation. I want to buy into the great plan that You have for me, and I recognize that this starts at the foot of the cross. I believe in my heart that Jesus died for my sins, that You raised Him from the dead, and that He is alive today. I confess with my mouth the lordship of Jesus Christ over my life. I receive Him today as my personal Lord and Savior. I ask You to please forgive me of all my sins and wash me clean. I believe that I am now saved, and that You are my Daddy in Heaven. In Jesus' name I pray.

Love,

____

Letter #20:

The Baptism in the Holy Spirit

Dear ____,

(your name here)

I love you, and I desire for you to live life in the fullness that I have planned for you. Today's letter will bring you understanding on the baptism in the Holy Spirit. There has been much confusion in this area, and I desire the very best for you, so please open your heart and receive My instruction.

As God, I have three distinct parts to My personality. I am God the Father, God the Son, and God the Holy Spirit. The Holy Spirit is the Spirit of your Father and of your Savior, Jesus. I desire for My character and power to be made known on the earth so that everyone can experience My goodness and grace. My children are My agents on the earth so that I can manifest Myself to everyone through their lives. In My divine wisdom, I have given the baptism or infilling of the Holy Spirit to fill My children to overflowing with My power and ability so that they can pour it out to others.

Many people say that the only filling with the Spirit that you receive is at salvation, but this is incorrect. I can prove to you with many examples from My Word that the baptism in the Spirit is an event separate from salvation, and I will provide two such examples in this letter.

Example 1: According to Romans 10:10, what are the requirements for salvation? There are only two: First, confess with your mouth that Jesus is Lord, and second believe in your heart that I raised Him from the dead. According to My Word, these are the only two requirements for salvation.

Many people say that the disciples were not saved until the day of Pentecost. They say that the "baptism in the Spirit" on that day was actually the seal of the Spirit that accompanies salvation. I will prove from My Word that this is incorrect, and that they had two distinct experiences with the Holy Spirit, one being the seal received at salvation and the other being the baptism received afterward.

Numerous times in the gospels the disciples confessed Jesus as Lord. They believed that He was the Messiah, confessed His lordship over their lives, and in so doing, they met the first requirement of salvation before Jesus' death on the cross. They could not meet the second requirement of believing in their hearts that I had raised Him from the dead until after His bodily resurrection. When Jesus, the risen Savior, appeared to the disciples after His resurrection as recorded in John 20, they believed that it was He and at that moment they met the second requirement and received their salvation. My Word says that He breathed on them and said, "Receive the Holy Spirit" (John 20:22). This was the seal of the Holy Spirit that enters a believer at the time of salvation. My Word also says that on the day of Pentecost they "were filled with the Holy Spirit" (Acts 2:4). How could the Holy Spirit fill them at the day of Pentecost if they were already full from the experience with Jesus in John 20? He could not; therefore, the baptism in the Spirit is a further experience with the Spirit that occurs in addition to salvation.

Example #2: In Acts 8, Philip traveled to minister the gospel to the people of Samaria. The Samaritans believed the gospel and received salvation under Philip's ministry. Philip then returned to Jerusalem and told the apostles and the Jewish church that the Gentile Samaritans had received salvation by faith in Jesus Christ. Upon hearing the news, Peter and John went to Samaria to visit their new brothers and sisters in the faith.

When the apostles from Jerusalem arrived in Samaria, they prayed that the Samaritan believers might receive the Holy Spirit, and they were baptized or filled with the Spirit immediately. My child, if the fullness of the Holy Spirit is received at the moment of salvation, then why would the apostles pray for them to receive the Spirit? Of course they would not, so the Spirit infilling that is referred to in this passage is an impartation separate from what is received at the moment of salvation. When Peter and John prayed for them, they received the impartation of My Spirit known in My Word as the baptism in the Holy Spirit.

My child, I have now clearly shown you with two examples from My Word that the baptism in the Spirit is a separate event that occurs in addition to salvation. The purpose of the baptism in the Holy Spirit is to fill believers with My power to witness and to do the same miraculous works that Jesus did. The baptism in the Holy Spirit is for every believer, and receiving it is the simplest thing in the world. Simply ask Me to fill you and believe that it is done when you ask. You will then be filled with My Spirit, no matter what you feel. Once you are filled with the Holy Spirit, My power and ability will begin to flow in your life in a greater measure.

My Word says that a tree is known by its fruit. When you are born again and sealed with the Spirit at salvation, the fruit of the Spirit should begin to manifest in your life. As you surrender to the Holy Spirit, He will be able to cultivate His fruit in you. The fruit of your life will be a blessing to others. The more you surrender, the greater the harvest of fruit in your life. When you become baptized in the Spirit, you are empowered to use His gifts in a greater measure. As you grow strong in Him, they will pour forth from you as a blessing to others. In order to operate in them, you must simply ask the Holy Spirit to use you to minister His gifts and believe that He will do what you ask. He will lead and guide you, and if you surrender to Him; He will use you mightily with His gifts.

The Holy Spirit is a precious gift. He is My presence with you on earth. He will speak the Word to your heart and give you revelation. He will guide you into all truth. He is the voice of your Daddy speaking to your heart. Please go to My Word and discover My plan for the ministry of the Spirit in your life. Please receive Him in all of His fullness. I love you and I'm with you by My Spirit.

Love,

Dad

Words from the Father's Heart

John 14:16-17—"And I will ask the Father (Daddy), and he will give you another Counselor to be with you forever—the Spirit of truth.The world cannot accept him, because it neither sees him nor knows him.But you know him, for he lives with you and will be in you."

John 16:7,13—"But I tell you the truth: It is for your good that I am going away. Unless I go away, the Counselor will not come to you; but if I go, I will send him to you . . . But when he, the Spirit of truth, comes, he will guide you into all truth. He will not speak on his own; he will speak only what he hears, and he will tell you what is yet to come."

John 7:38-39—"'Whoever believes in me, as the Scripture has said, streams of living water will flow from within him.' By this he meant the Spirit, whom those who believed in him were later to receive. Up to that time the Spirit had not been given, since Jesus had not yet been glorified."

John 20:19-23—"On the evening of that first day of the week, when the disciples were together, with the doors locked for fear of the Jews, Jesus came and stood among them and said, 'Peace be with you!' After he said this, he showed them his hands and side. The disciples were overjoyed when they saw the Lord. Again Jesus said, 'Peace be with you! As the Father (Daddy) has sent me, I am sending you.' And with that he breathed on them and said, 'Receive the Holy Spirit. If you forgive anyone his sins, they are forgiven; if you do not forgive them, they are not forgiven.'"

Acts 1:8—"But you will receive power when the Holy Spirit comes on you; and you will be my witnesses in Jerusalem, and in all Judea and Samaria, and to the ends of the earth."

Acts 2:2-4—"Suddenly a sound like the blowing of a violent wind came from heaven and filled the whole house where they were sitting. They saw what seemed to be tongues of fire that separated and came to rest on each of them. All of them were filled with the Holy Spirit and began to speak in other tongues as the Spirit enabled them."

Acts 4:31—"After they prayed, the place where they were meeting was shaken. And they were all filled with the Holy Spirit and spoke the word of God (Daddy) boldly."

Questions from the Father's Heart

1) Have you received the baptism of the Holy Spirit in addition to your salvation? ______________________________

____

____

____

____

____

2) How do you think the infilling of the Holy Spirit should change your life personally? ______________________________

____

____

____

____

____

3) How can you begin to allow the Holy Spirit to cultivate His fruit more in your life?________________________

____

____

____

____

____

4) Ask the Holy Spirit to reveal what gifts He has given you. As He does, how can you begin to allow Him to pour His gifts through you to bless others? ________________

____

____

____

____

____

Prayer to the Father

Daddy,

Thank You so much for the wonderful gift of the Holy Spirit. He is my Comforter and Counselor, my Strength, my Help, and my Song. Precious Holy Spirit, I surrender to Your work in my life. Please cultivate Your fruit in the garden of my life, and bring forth an abundant harvest of it to bless others. Please reveal to me the gifts that You have imparted to me, and use me to pour those gifts out as a blessing to those around me. I love You! In Jesus' name I pray.

Love,

____

Identifying with My Father

I am empowered by the Holy Spirit to be a bold witness for Jesus and to do the same works He did.

(Now, add your own thoughts.)

Prayer to Receive the Baptism in the Holy Spirit

Daddy,

As I was reading this letter, I realized that I have never received the baptism in the Holy Spirit. Thank You so much for not only giving me the gift of salvation, but for pouring out Your Spirit to live inside me. Just like I received my salvation by faith, I ask You right now to baptize me in the precious Holy Spirit. I believe that I am now baptized in the Spirit. Precious Holy Spirit, I surrender to Your work in my life. Please cultivate your fruit in the garden of my life, and bring forth an abundant harvest of it to bless others. Please reveal to me the gifts that You have imparted to me, and use me to pour those gifts out as a blessing to those around me. I love You! In Jesus' name I pray.

Love,

____

Letter #21: Faith

Dearest Child ______________________________,

(your name here)

Please come sit with Me while I teach you today about faith. My darling, I love you so very dearly. As you have grown to learn more about Me, you have heard much teaching on the subject of faith. Bless your heart, I know that you have been confused on what faith really is, how to get it, and how to use it. Today I am going to clear up this confusion for you so that you can go forward and exercise the wonderful gift of faith I have placed in you to obtain all the goodness that I desire for you to possess.

My child, there is much teaching regarding faith that is contrary to My written Word. I am troubled as I hear others teach you things about faith that are not in line with the principles clearly laid out in my Word. Dearest child, let's go together to My Word and find out the truth about faith.

My love, I am right here to answer all your questions, and the most important question is, "What is faith?" Simply stated, faith is the ability to believe. It can be compared to intelligence, because intelligence is the ability to learn, and faith, its spiritual equivalent, is the ability to believe. Everyone has a certain level of intelligence, and similarly, everyone also has the measure of faith. The level of intelligence varies between individuals based on My plan for a person, but everyone has been given the same measure of faith. What is the measure of faith that I have given to every person? It is the same measure that Jesus was given when He became a man and walked the earth.

To begin understanding how to apply our definition of faith, refer back to the example of intelligence for a moment. Remember that everyone is born with a certain level of intelligence or ability to learn. Throughout life a person must make choices as to how they will apply their intelligence to benefit from it. For example, in college a person chooses to apply their intelligence to a course of study that determines their career path. Some people study medicine and become doctors. Others study law and become lawyers. In each case, a person molds the fresh clay of intelligence they are given into the pattern of their choosing.

The application of faith works very similar to that of intelligence. When faith is applied it becomes belief. Everyone is given the measure of faith and must choose the set of beliefs that they will mold their faith into. For example, some people choose to believe in Jesus, My Son, and receive the gift of salvation. Others choose to believe that I do not exist and are lost. Still others believe in their money and are consumed by greed. All of these people have faith, or the ability to believe, in equal measure. The difference is, the choices they have made in applying their faith has given each of them a different set of beliefs. Similarly, every person is responsible for taking their faith clay that I have given them and forming it into a set of beliefs.

To give you greater understanding, I will give you a lesson from Greek, the original language of the New Testament, concerning the word "faith." The Greek noun for "faith" is *pistis*. The Greek verb for "belief" is *pisteuo*. "Unbelief" and "not believe" are formed by adding an "a" in front of the root words to make *apistis* and *apisteuo*. *Pisteuo, apistis,* and *apisteuo* are almost exclusively translated "believe," "unbelief," and "not believe" throughout the New Testament. The one word in this family that is translated differently is *pistis*. It is almost always translated "faith" rather than "belief." This is inconsistent with the translation of the three other words in the same family. In almost all cases in the New Testament, a better translation of *pistis* is "belief" rather than "faith," and consistency in translation would virtually eliminate the word "faith" from the New Testament and replace it with the word "belief."

A consistent translation of My Word would make it easier for you to grasp the true meaning of faith. Faith seems so mystical to many, mainly because it has had an incorrect definition associated with it. Belief, on the other hand, is a very simple concept. It is complete and wholehearted trust in something. This takes all the mystery out of faith. Faith is the ability to believe. Belief is whole-hearted trust in something.

This new definition of faith eliminates the need for the question, "How do I obtain faith?" The answer to the question is that you already possess all the faith that you are ever going to have. The real question is, "How do I mold my belief in the Word to the level that Jesus possessed while on earth?" My child, the answer to this question is very simple. Romans 10 translated with our new definition of faith says, "Belief comes from hearing the message, and the message is heard through the word of Christ." This simply means that hearing My Word will form your faith into beliefs about Me that are consistent with My nature and My Word. My Word will form your faith into a bridge of belief that will connect My supernatural Kingdom to the natural world that you live in.

Dearest child, faith is not difficult. All you must do is apply your faith to My Word and believe that I am who I say I am, and that I will do what I say I will do. Please allow My Holy Spirit to put your faith on the potter's wheel and mold it into a vessel that will contain an overflowing abundance of My power and ability. I love you!

Love,

Dad

Words from the Father's Heart

Hebrews 11:1—"Now faith is being sure of what we hope for and certain of what we do not see."

Romans 12:3—"For by the grace given me I say to every one of you: Do not think of yourself more highly than you ought, but rather think of yourself with sober judgment, in accordance with the measure of faith God (Daddy) has given you."

2 Corinthians 5:7—"We live by faith, not by sight."

Romans 10:17—"Consequently, faith comes from hearing the message, and the message is heard through the word of Christ."

Mark 11:22-24—"'Have faith in God (Daddy),' Jesus answered. 'I tell you the truth, if anyone says to this mountain, "Go, throw yourself into the sea," and does not doubt in his heart but believes that what he says will happen, it will be done for him. Therefore I tell you, whatever you ask for in prayer, believe that you have received it, and it will be yours.'"

Matthew 17:20—"He replied, 'Because you have so little faith. I tell you the truth, if you have faith as small as a mustard seed, you can say to this mountain, "Move from here to there" and it will move. Nothing will be impossible for you.'"

Questions from the Father's Heart

1) How has this letter changed your view of faith? ________

2) What misconceptions have you had about faith and how it works? ________

3) How do you feel now about how simple it is to believe Me and My Word? ________

____

____

____

____

4) How will this letter help you to more easily walk in faith or belief?____

____

____

____

____

5) What will you do to begin applying the principles you have learned here to your life today? ______________________

____

____

____

____

____

PRAYER TO THE FATHER

Daddy,

Thank You so much for writing this letter for me to clear up my understanding of the concept of faith. I have struggled to understand how I am supposed to stand in faith and believe You and Your Word. This letter has cleared up my misunderstanding, and now I see how simple it is to believe You. Please help me to apply what I have learned, and mold my belief until my life conforms to Your Word completely just like Jesus. Mature the faith that You have given me in Your Word until I believe Your Word before I will believe anything else. I love You! In Jesus' name I pray.

Love,

____

Identifying with My Father

With my Heavenly Daddy's help I am molding my faith into unshakeable belief in His Word.

(Now, add your own thoughts.)

Letter #22: Righteousness—Your Position in Christ

Dear __________________________________,

(your name here)

My child, in a previous letter I very clearly unfolded My plan of salvation to you. Today I want to introduce a new idea to you, which will build upon the principles you learned in that letter. Before you accepted Jesus as your Lord and Savior, you were alive, yet you were completely dead to Me because of sin. We could have no fellowship because your very nature was sinful and impure. When you accepted Jesus as your Lord and Savior, I removed your sinful nature from your spirit man and gave you a new nature. This new nature is My nature and is called "righteousness."

When you accepted Jesus as Savior, you became clothed with My nature and thus gained right standing with Me. This right standing, or "righteous nature," gives you your place as My child with the ability to stand in My presence as though sin had never touched your life. So when I say that you are My righteousness in Christ, it has two meanings. It means that you have taken on My pure, or "righteous," nature, and that you can fellowship with Me as though you never had a sin nature.

My child, let Me give you an example that will illustrate this clearly. Picture My royal throne room in Heaven with Me sitting in majesty on the throne of the universe. Jesus is seated at My right hand as the heir of all things. He has been given all authority in Heaven and on earth according to My Word. Now, My child, visualize another throne right beside Jesus. Who does that one belong to? That throne belongs to you, for you are seated in Heavenly places at the right hand of Jesus!

When you were dead in sin, I raised you up and made you to sit with Christ Jesus in My Heavenly Kingdom. Do you think that a sin-stained person could dare to show their face in My royal throne room, much less sit with the royalty on a throne? Never! My child, you must learn to see yourself through the eyes of who My Word says you are. When you were born again, the sin nature was removed from your heart. You took on My righteous nature at that moment. You are clothed with a royal robe of righteousness in My sight. Upon your head sits a royal crown symbolizing the authority that you bear in My Kingdom. You are not filthy and sin-stained; you are washed whiter than snow in My eyes.

How does this translate into the natural? Remember Jesus' words before He ascended to Heaven? He said, "All authority in heaven and on earth has been given to me" (Matthew 28:18). All the authority that He had, He gave to you. How could I possibly expect you to do what Jesus did, and reflect who Jesus was if I did not give you the tools to do the job? I have filled you with the same Holy Spirit that He had when He was on the earth. I have given you the same authority and ability in Me that He had to accomplish the works that I have laid out for you. I have given this to you for you to declare My Kingdom in truth and power.

Imagine for a moment the following scenario in the natural: What if I was your earthly father, and I was absolute ruler of a kingdom on earth? What if I gave you the same authority in My kingdom that I had? When you spoke, it was just like Me speaking. When you acted, it was just like Me acting. Imagine your attitude and how you would act if this were the case. If you came across something that you did not like, something that you knew would not please Me, then you would simply give the command and it would be changed. You would speak and act with authority, like you were in charge. My child, this simple example literally illustrates what I have done in the realm of the spirit concerning My Kingdom on earth. In Christ I have given you the same authority and ability that He had on earth.

You must begin to see yourself through the eyes of My Word. You are not a sinner. You have My very nature inside you. Dare to begin to walk in My authority and ability in your life, and watch Me go to work for you when you step up to take what is rightfully yours. Begin to go to the Word and discover your rights and privileges in Christ. Ask your Helper, the Holy Spirit, to open your eyes to the reality of your righteousness and what it means to you. Begin to visualize yourself in My throne room in Heaven, for you are seated together in Heavenly places in Christ. Hold your head up and act like a child of the King!

From the throne room position in Christ that I have shown you, I want you to begin to look at the problems of life that you have been facing. How do they begin to look now? Go to My Word and find a promise that applies to your situation and use that promise to change the situation. Act like you have total authority over that thing that is not in line with My Word, and deal with it just like you would deal with something that was out of line in the example of the earthly kingdom.

My child, as you begin to exercise your authority and your position in Christ, you will see your life line up more and more with My Kingdom plan for you. I love you dearly, and I am always here to help you reach out and take what I have given you in Christ.

Love,

Dad

Words from the Father's Heart

Matthew 28:18-20—"Then Jesus came to them and said, 'All authority in heaven and on earth has been given to me. Therefore go and make disciples of all nations, baptizing them in the name of the Father (Daddy) and of the Son and of the Holy Spirit, and teaching them to obey everything I have commanded you. And surely I am with you always, to the very end of the age.'"

2 Corinthians 5:17-21—"Therefore, if anyone is in Christ, he is a new creation; the old has gone, the new has come! All this is from God (Daddy), who reconciled us to himself through Christ and gave us the ministry of reconciliation: that God (Daddy) was reconciling the world to himself in Christ, not counting men's sins against them. And he has committed to us the message of reconciliation. We are therefore Christ's ambassadors, as though God (Daddy) were making his appeal through us. We implore you on Christ's behalf: Be reconciled to God (Daddy). God (Daddy) made him who had no sin to be sin for us, so that in him we might become the righteousness of God (Daddy)."

Ephesians 2:4-6—"But because of his great love for us, God (Daddy), who is rich in mercy, made us alive with Christ even when we were dead in transgressions—it is by grace you have been saved. And God (Daddy) raised us up with Christ and seated us with him in the heavenly realms in Christ Jesus."

2 Peter 1:2-4—"Grace and peace be yours in abundance through the knowledge of God (Daddy) and of Jesus our Lord. His divine power has given us everything we need for life and Godliness through our knowledge of him who called us by his own glory and goodness. Through these he has given us his very great and precious promises, so that through them you may participate in the divine nature and escape the corruption in the world caused by evil desires."

Ephesians 1:3—"Praise be to the God and Father (Daddy) of our Lord Jesus Christ, who has blessed us in the heavenly realms with every spiritual blessing in Christ."

John 14:12-14—"I tell you the truth, anyone who has faith in me will do what I have been doing. He will do even greater things than these, because I am going to the Father

(Daddy)..And I will do whatever you ask in my name, so that the Son may bring glory to the Father (Daddy).You may ask me for anything in my name, and I will do it."

Questions from the Father's Heart

1) How has this letter changed your image of yourself in Christ? ______________________________

2) What does this teaching on righteousness mean to you and your life? ______________________________

3) How will you begin to apply this principle of who you are and your position in Christ to your life? ______________________________

4) Meditate on some situations and circumstances that you face. By seeing yourself in My throne room and walking in your authority in Christ, how are you now able to deal with those things? ______________________________

____

____

____

____

____

____

Prayer to the Father

Daddy,

Thank You so much for giving me Your righteous nature and for giving me right standing in Your sight. Please help me to apply the principles I have learned in this letter to begin obtaining the inheritance that You have given me in Christ. Help me to grow and mature in Christ daily, so that I honor You and the position that You have given me as Your child. Help me begin to live my life with a vision of my place in Your Heavenly throne room. Please help me to walk in the authority and righteousness that You have given me. I love You! In Jesus' name I pray.

Love,

____

Identifying with My Father

I see myself as my Heavenly Daddy sees me,
seated on a throne in His Heavenly kingdom.

(Now, add your own thoughts.)

Letter #23: Prayer

My Dearest Child ______________________,
(your name here)

I love you with all My heart, and I enjoy fellowshipping with you so much. As you continue to apply the principles I taught you about our relationship, you will draw closer and closer in fellowship with Me. My child, prayer plays a vital role in a healthy relationship with Me, and I want you to understand what prayer is and how to pray so that you can succeed in your spiritual walk. Contrary to what you have been taught, prayer is not something that is difficult or hard to do. It is simply talking to and fellowshipping with Me, and this includes bringing needs to Me and asking Me to meet them. Since the focus of the entire first section of letters is on fellowship with Me, this prayer letter will focus on the operation of your faith (or belief) to get your requests answered.

My child, asking and receiving are simply extensions of your fellowship with Me. When you need something I want you to just come to Me and ask. I said in My Word that as your Heavenly Father, I will give you good gifts if you will just ask Me. I also said that I will meet every one of your needs with abundance, and I know what you need before you ever ask. My written Word contains My will for every aspect of your life. I have made promises that cover every situation and circumstance that you could possibly face. When you pray a prayer that is based on what I have already revealed as My will, then My answer to your prayer is always "yes." This puts responsibility on you to go to My Word and learn to form your prayers based on the promises that I have given you. When you do this, you will receive a "yes" answer to every prayer that you pray. Sometimes you will have to wait for Me to move circumstances on your behalf, but the answer to your prayer is still always "yes," as long as it is prayed in line with My Word.

Many times in the Word you will find that your big brother, Jesus, said whatever you ask Me in His name will be given to you. He also said that whatever things you desire, believe that you receive them when you pray for them, and you will have them.

My child, I am going to give you a very simple example of how to view your requests to Me on behalf of yourself and others. Let's imagine an example of a father and his child. If the child were to go to the father and ask for a new toy, the father might say something like, "Of course, little one, I will buy that toy for you." In this case, the request would be made and granted at the same time. At the moment the little child asks and the father says "yes," then it is as good as done.

Now, what if the child went back to the father the next day and made the same request again? He would again say "yes" to the child's request. What if the child went back the next day and made the same request? By this time the father would begin to think that the child either did not understand or did not believe what he had said about buying the toy.

My child, I feel the same way when My children keep coming back to Me and asking Me to meet the same need over and over and over. In some cases, My children do not understand My heart and how My Word operates. In other cases, they do not believe that I heard and answered their requests the first time they asked. When you pray and ask Me to do something for you, I hear and answer that request the first time you ask.

My child, remember the lessons that I taught you about faith. How do you get anything from your Heavenly Dad? According to James, you must ask Me from a heart of belief; otherwise, your prayer will not get answered, because your belief in Me and My ability allows Me to move on the requests that you make. It allows Me to act and perform on your behalf. If you do not know what My answer to your request is going to be when you ask, then how can you ask in belief? You must know My will in order to be fully assured that your request will be granted; otherwise, you have no basis for belief that I will answer your prayer.

My child, you must not think that you can pray a prayer, saying, "Father if it is Your will to grant this request, then please answer it, but if not, then I will accept this as Your will." On the surface this seems like a very legitimate way to pray, but let Me show you the fallacy here. I have clearly laid out My will in My Word concerning everything in your life. I have declared that in order to receive from Me, you must ask and believe that you will get what you are asking for according to My Word. If you are unsure of what My Word says when you pray, then you will not be able to truly stand in My definition of belief for your request to be granted, and you are therefore asking in unbelief.

My child, please do not think that if you do not know what to ask for, then you cannot pray. Goodness, no!! You can come to Me anytime and ask for My wisdom, guidance, and instruction. You must begin to form your prayers carefully and in line with My Word. When you do not know My will in a situation, please come to Me and ask Me to show you My will so that you can pray accurately. Please refer to My letter about hearing My voice; it teaches you how I will answer your prayer for wisdom and guidance for your life.

As I bring this letter to a close, I will give you some practical instruction that will help you begin learning to pray in line with My Word. Often My children waste many words by praying about things over and over or by repeating themselves with many words. Remember that I said in My Word that you will not be heard in prayer for your many words. A believing prayer does not have to be long; it needs to be direct and to the point. When you come to Me to pray about something, please first ask for My direction on how to pray, and then go to My Word to find out what it says about your situation or circumstance. Once you find My will in My Word, you can pray effectively on this basis.

Now, child, I want you to begin writing down your prayers in a notebook. Take time to formulate them accurately and exactly the way you want them written. Ask Me for My help. It would be My pleasure. Once you have the prayer in the form that you want it, then you can come to Me in true belief because you are praying in line with My Word. Then pray that prayer just like you were the little child asking daddy for a toy in the example I gave you previously. Once you have done this, then My answer to your prayer is "yes" according to My Word.

After you pray, I want you to see that prayer as though you already have the answer to it. Picture yourself in your mind like the child with the toy already in hand. When you pray, it is done! My dear child, prayer is not hard or difficult; it is My gift that allows you to tap into My ability. I love you and I want to give good things to you. Be free in your prayer life, My child. It is My good pleasure to give you all the things of My Kingdom.

Love,

Dad

Words from the Father's Heart

Matthew 7:7-11—"Ask and it will be given to you; seek and you will find; knock and the door will be opened to you. For everyone who asks receives; he who seeks finds; and to him who knocks, the door will be opened. Which of you, if his son asks for bread, will give him a stone? Or if he asks for a fish, will give him a snake? If you, then, though you are evil, know how to give good gifts to your children, how much more will your Father (Daddy) in Heaven give good gifts to those who ask him!"

Philippians 4:19—"And my God (Daddy) will meet all your needs according to his glorious riches in Christ Jesus."

2 Corinthians 1:20—"For no matter how many promises God (Daddy) has made, they are "Yes" in Christ. And so through him the "Amen" is spoken by us to the glory of God (Daddy)."

1 John 5:14-15—"This is the confidence we have in approaching God (Daddy): that if we ask anything according to his will, he hears us. And if we know that he hears us—whatever we ask—we know that we have what we asked of him."

James 1:5-8—"If any of you lacks wisdom, he should ask God (Daddy), who gives generously to all without finding fault, and it will be given to him.But when he asks, he must believe and not doubt, because he who doubts is like a wave of the sea, blown and tossed by the wind. That man should not think he will receive anything from the Lord; he is a double-minded man, unstable in all he does."

Matthew 21:18-22—"Early in the morning, as he was on his way back to the city, he was hungry. Seeing a fig tree by the road, he went up to it but found nothing on it except leaves. Then he said to it, 'May you never bear fruit again!' Immediately the tree withered. When the disciples saw this, they were amazed. 'How did the fig tree wither so quickly?' they asked. Jesus replied, 'I tell you the truth, if you have faith and do not doubt, not only can you do what was done to the fig tree, but also you can say to this mountain, "Go, throw yourself into the sea," and it will be done. If you believe, you will receive whatever you ask for in prayer.'"

Matthew 18:19-20—"Again, I tell you that if two of you on earth agree about anything you ask for, it will be done for you by my Father (Daddy) in Heaven. For where two or three come together in my name, there am I with them."

Questions from the Father's Heart

1) How has the vision I gave you of us walking together hand in hand as Father and child impacted your prayer life? ____________________

2) How does this letter change your ideas about what prayer is and how to pray? ____________________

3) How will you apply what you have learned here to your prayer life so that you can begin to see the answers to your prayers that you desire? ____________________

4) In your notebook that I asked you to start, make a list of things you need to pray about. Keep this notebook with your Bible so that you can continually remind yourself about the things you are believing Me for.

Prayer to the Father

Daddy,

Thank You for the relationship that You have shown me I can have with You. Thank You for showing me that prayer is not something hard or burdensome. I see now that prayer is simply talking to You, sharing my heart and my feelings, and asking You to meet my needs. Help me to pray with a heart full of belief in Your Word so that I can get every need I pray about met. From now on, every time I pray a prayer I will see it as though I already have the answer as soon as I pray. I believe You to perform Your Word on my behalf. I love You! In Jesus' name I pray.

Love,

____

Identifying with My Father

I pray my Heavenly Daddy's will by praying according to His Word. *(Now, add your own thoughts.)*

Letter #24: Healing

Dear ________________________________,

(your name here)

In My great love for you I have clearly laid out My will in My Word concerning every aspect of your life. As I taught you in an earlier letter, once I speak something, it is forever settled. I have a divine plan to bring you prosperity and wholeness in every area of life, including your physical health and well-being. Today I want to teach you how to use My Word and its promises to obtain the health and healing that I desire for you.

My child, while on the earth, Jesus was a perfect representation of both My will and My person. He spoke My heart, and His words are the same yesterday, today, and forever. In Matthew chapter 8, there is an account of a leper who came to Jesus to see if Jesus would heal him. The man said, "Lord, if you are willing, you can make me clean" (v. 2). Jesus touched the man and said, "I am willing. Be clean!" (v. 3). The man was instantly cleansed of his leprosy. The man was certain that Jesus had the ability to heal him, but he did not know if the Master was willing. Jesus, once and for all, answered the question of My willingness to heal when He answered this man's question. I am both willing and able to heal just as much now as when Jesus spoke so long ago.

When He walked the earth, Jesus was a man. He was only able to touch and heal a certain number of people because of physical limitations. The shedding of His blood and His resurrection from the dead made the same healing virtue that flowed through Jesus' hands available to any of My children who believe that they possess it. First Peter 2:24 says, "By his wounds you have been healed." "Have been healed" is a past tense verb meaning that your healing was accomplished by Jesus at the time of His death and resurrection. He bore all sickness and disease so that you do not have to bear any at all.

When sickness or infirmity tries to attack your body, you must understand and believe that health and healing belong to you. You must then act upon what you know to be true, even though you may not feel healthy and healed. The truth is that you are healed and healthy according to your covenant with Me. The facts may be that you feel sick, but you must choose what you are going to believe. Often Jesus said words like, "According to your faith (belief) will it be done to you." Will you choose to believe the truth of My Word, or will you choose to believe the facts of what you see or feel? You will establish in your life whichever one you choose to believe.

Now dear child, picture yourself at My right hand like I showed you in the letter on your position in Christ. See yourself clothed with My robe of righteousness signifying My righteous nature. Picture yourself again with a royal crown on your head signifying the authority of My Kingdom. Now, picture some sickness trying to afflict you as you are seated in My throne room. What are you going to do about it? I have given you the same authority that Jesus had on the earth. My child, stand up from your throne, point your finger at sickness and say, "In the name of Jesus which is above every name, I command you to cease your affliction and leave my body now. By Jesus' stripes I have been healed and you are trespassing in my body. I will not tolerate you. Leave me now, in the name of Jesus, and do not return."

Dear child, this is how you must deal with all physical affliction. If a sickness or affliction tries to attack you or a loved one, speak to it like I just taught you. If it does not leave the first time you command it, then keep speaking to it until it bows its knee to the name of Jesus and My Word is manifest. As your confidence in your authority grows, you will more easily shake off things that come against you.

I love you, My child, and I have made provision in My covenant for you to never live sick another day in your life. Ask your Helper, the Holy Spirit, to give you a revelation of My will concerning your physical health. Ask Him to help you to grow in belief until you are able to cast off any physical sickness or infirmity that would attempt to assail you. I love you, and I am always with you.

Love,

Dad

Words from the Father's Heart

Matthew 8:2-4—"A man with leprosy came and knelt before him and said, 'Lord, if you are willing, you can make me clean.' Jesus reached out his hand and touched the man. 'I am willing,' he said. 'Be clean!' Immediately he was cured of his leprosy."

Hebrews 13:8—"Jesus Christ is the same yesterday and today and forever."

Isaiah 53:5—"But he was pierced for our transgressions, he was crushed for our iniquities; the punishment that brought us peace was upon him, and by his wounds we are healed."

1 Peter 2:24—"He himself bore our sins in his body on the tree, so that we might die to sins and live for righteousness; by his wounds you have been healed."

Mark 16:17-18—"And these signs will accompany those who believe: In my name they will drive out demons; they will speak in new tongues; they will pick up snakes with their hands; and when they drink deadly poison, it will not hurt them at all; they will place their hands on sick people, and they will get well."

Psalm 107:20—"He sent forth his word and healed them; he rescued them from the grave."

Acts 10:38—"How God (Daddy) anointed Jesus of Nazareth with the Holy Spirit and power, and how he went around doing good and healing all who were under the power of the devil, because God (Daddy) was with him."

QUESTIONS FROM THE FATHER'S HEART

1) How has this letter changed your ideas about physical sickness and infirmity in the body of a believer? ________

2) Are you or someone you know suffering from some sort of physical infirmity? ________

3) What are you going to do about this physical affliction that has attacked your/their body? ________

4) What steps can you take to apply what you have learned in this letter to your life today? ________

5) How can you use My Word not only to receive healing for yourself and others, but also to prevent physical affliction from coming again? (Hint: Speak the Word!)____________

____

____

____

____

Prayer to the Father

Daddy,

Thank You so much for teaching me that I do not have to put up with any sort of physical affliction, and for teaching me how to deal with these works of the enemy. Please help me get the revelation of Your will for physical health and well-being down in my heart so I can believe You for health and healing for myself and for those around me. As You help me, I will be diligent to apply what You have taught me to my life. I will put Your Word in my heart and in my mouth so that no sickness or affliction can come upon me or those I love. Please help me to see myself through Your eyes, and deal with every sickness, affliction, or infirmity from my position seated at the right hand of Jesus in Your throne room. I love You! In Jesus' name I pray.

Love,

____

Identifying with My Father

Physical health and wholeness are part of my covenant of salvation with my Heavenly Daddy.

(Now, add your own thoughts.)

Prayer for Healing

Daddy,

I have been being afflicted in my body, and I need Your healing touch. According to Your Word, I have already been healed by the stripes that Jesus took for me. Right now I receive the healing and restoration in my body that You have provided for me. I believe that I am healed regardless of what I see or feel. Thank You for my healing and for bringing it into full manifestation in my body. In Jesus name I pray.

Love,

Dearest ________________________________,
(your name here)

As I have told you in previous letters, My great love for you has made provision for your well-being in every area of life. I love you so much, and I want you to flourish and prosper at all times. My child, no loving parent wants any hurt or harm to come to their children, and because you are My pride and joy, I too desire for you to be safe from all harm every minute of every day. I am your loving Father, and I have given you many promises of My protection so that you can live your life without fear of hurt or destruction. Today I am going to teach you how to tap into the protection and safekeeping that I have provided for you and those you love in the covenant I have made with you through the blood of Jesus.

Dearest heart, Jesus said that nothing shall harm you in any way, but this promise depends upon you doing your part. Let's look together at Jesus' words in Luke 10:19: "I have given you authority to trample on snakes and scorpions and to overcome all the power of the enemy; nothing will harm you." Here Jesus gives you authority over anything that would bring you harm, and He implies that if you exercise this authority over the forces of darkness, then nothing will be able to harm you in any way.

To better understand what Jesus meant, let's look at the following example. Suppose that a loving father gave his son a brand-new car as a high school graduation present. He hands the keys over to him on graduation day and says, "This car now belongs to you. If you want to go anywhere, just get in it and go!" It makes sense that from that point forward if the boy is going to go anywhere, then he will be responsible for using the car that his dad has given him to get there. It would be silly if he wanted to go to a movie with a friend to go ask his dad to drive him! Why? The father has given the authority for the use of that car to his son.

Likewise, the same is true of your authority over the forces of darkness that would seek to bring hurt or harm to you or your loved ones. Jesus has given you the right to use all of His authority as though it were your own. In the verse from Luke 10:19, Jesus is saying that if you will use the authority He has given you, then nothing will be able to harm you in any way.

As a second example, let's pretend that I am the king of the most powerful nation on earth. As My child, you are My royal ambassador to other nations. When you go out to other nations, you go in My place representing Me as though I were there, and all My authority and power are behind you. When you speak, people listen and obey because of the authority that you have behind you. My child, I think you can see from this simple example that I am the great King over all the earth, and you are My royal ambassador on earth. You have been given My authority to use, and when you speak My

Words on earth, it is just as though I were there speaking. You stand in My authority as long as you stand upon My Word.

My child, I have made it clear in My Word that safety and protection are your covenant rights as My child. Let's return again to the throne room illustration to learn how to enjoy the protection I promised for you and your loved ones. As you see yourself seated on a throne at Jesus' right hand, make a list of people that you desire to see covered by My hand of protection. Please include not only persons, but also property, ministries, etc. in this list. Include those who are not saved whom you desire to see come to salvation, for at your petition I am able to extend My merciful hand to cover even those who have no covenant with Me.

Now visualize yourself and all those you are petitioning for gathered around My throne. In your mind, turn to face Me, and express to Me your desire for My protection according to the promises found in My Word. Imagine My hand covering all of you so that you are protected in My secret place. Visualize My supernatural wall of protection that no weapon can penetrate encircling you. You and those you pray for are covered by My protection and nothing can harm you if you will exercise both the authority I have given you and your belief in My Word.

If you will begin to visualize My Word the way I wrote it, then it will be much easier for you to exercise belief in My promises. It is important that you begin to pray prayers of protection over yourself and others daily so that you do not give any opportunity to the enemy who desires to bring you hurt and harm.

My dearest child, you have heard rumors and false teachings that your loving Heavenly Father will bring you trials and allow you harm to teach you things. Dear heart, nothing could be further from the truth. I have given you authority so that you can bring My power on the scene in your life. Just like the example of the teenager with the new car, I cannot step into the areas of your life that I have given you the authority in My Word to govern. Like the earthly father who gave the car keys to his son, I have given you the keys of authority over all the forces of darkness. If the devil is to be stopped in your life and in the lives of those you love, then it is your responsibility to do something about him and his works by standing in your rightful position in Christ. I cannot exercise the authority that I have given to you.

My child, as I close this letter, I will once and for all show you that I will never bring you any harm to teach you something or fail to extend My hand to protect you when you believe Me to do so. My Word makes it clear that I desire for you to be safe from all harm. If I used harm to teach you or refused you protection AT ANY TIME, then how could you ever stand in belief for My protection at all? Your belief or unwavering trust in My Word is contingent upon knowing that I will always do what I promised. The only way you can have unwavering trust or true belief is if you know beyond all doubt that I will do what I promised. If I promised protection from all harm, but occasionally refused to extend My protection or used hurt to teach you, then how could you have any basis for belief in My protection at any time? You could not!!!!! Therefore, any and all harm is never, ever from your Father

God but is a result of the works of darkness and of living in a world full of sin.

I have promised to keep you completely safe from ALL harm if you will simply believe My Word and exercise your authority. Please allow My Holy Spirit to teach you about the protection provided in My covenant with you. I love you, dear heart, and I will always protect and keep you safe. You are My world!!!!

Love

Dad

Words from the Father's Heart

Psalm 91—"He who dwells in the shelter of the Most High will rest in the shadow of the Almighty. I will say of the LORD (Daddy), 'He is my refuge and my fortress, my God (Daddy), in whom I trust.' Surely he will save you from the fowler's snare and from the deadly pestilence. He will cover you with his feathers, and under his wings you will find refuge; his faithfulness will be your shield and rampart. You will not fear the terror of night, nor the arrow that flies by day, nor the pestilence that stalks in the darkness, nor the plague that destroys at midday. A thousand may fall at your side, ten thousand at your right hand, but it will not come near you. You will only observe with your eyes and see the punishment of the wicked. If you make the Most High your dwelling—even the LORD (Daddy), who is my refuge—then no harm will befall you, no disaster will come near your tent. For he will command his angels concerning you to guard you in all your ways; they will lift you up in their hands, so that you will not strike your foot against a stone. You will tread upon the lion and the cobra; you will trample the great lion and the serpent. 'Because he loves me,' says the LORD (Daddy), 'I will rescue him; I will protect him, for he acknowledges my name. He will call upon me, and I will answer him; I will be with him in trouble, I will deliver him and honor him. With long life will I satisfy him and show him my salvation.'"

Isaiah 54:17—"'No weapon forged against you will prevail, and you will refute every tongue that accuses you. This is the heritage of the servants of the LORD (Daddy), and this is their vindication from me,' declares the LORD (Daddy)."

Luke 10:18-19—"He replied, 'I saw Satan fall like lightning from heaven. I have given you authority to trample on snakes and scorpions and to overcome all the power of the enemy; nothing will harm you.'"

Matthew 28:18-20—"Then Jesus came to them and said, 'All authority in heaven and on earth has been given to me. Therefore go and make disciples of all nations, baptizing them in the name of the Father (Daddy) and of the Son and of the Holy Spirit, and teaching them to obey everything I have commanded you. And surely I am with you always, to the very end of the age.'"

Questions from the Father's Heart

1) How has this letter changed your ideas about My provision for your protection and safekeeping? ____________

2) What are some faulty ideas that you have had about the protection that I have promised? ____________

3) How do the two examples I gave teach you how to use your authority so that you and those you love can enjoy My protection over your lives? ____________

4) How are you going to put into practice what I have taught you here for yourself and for your loved ones? ____________

PRAYER TO THE FATHER

Daddy,

Thank You so much for teaching me about Your plans and desires for protection and safekeeping for me and those I love. Thank You for giving me the authority and the responsibility to use Your Word to obtain Your many promises. Please help me to be diligent to pray Your protection and safekeeping around myself and those I love. As You help me, I will be diligent to stand against the schemes of the wicked one and believe You for Your protective hand to cover us all. I believe that nothing can harm us in any way if I properly use the authority that You have given me according to Your Word. I love You! In Jesus' name I pray.

Love,

____

IDENTIFYING WITH MY FATHER

Nothing can harm me or those I love because I stand in the authority that my Heavenly Daddy has given to me. *(Now, add your own thoughts.)*

Dear ______________________________________,

(your name here)

I love you dearly, and I desire the best for you in everything. The purpose of this entire series of letters has been to open your eyes to the great blessing I desire to pour out into your life as you put My Word to work. I have great plans to bring you what I call whole life prosperity and a bright future filled with hope. This letter will teach you how to obtain this prosperity through a revelation of My blessing and the principles of sowing and reaping.

My child, many people think that prosperity means being able to pay your bills or having some extra money in your pocket, but My definition of prosperity covers so much more than finances. True prosperity is having My blessing flowing in every area of your life. The word "blessed" is used often throughout My Word, and it means "empowered to prosper." My Word says in many places that you are blessed because you are My child and because of the covenant that we have. In fact, our covenant is a covenant of blessing. Read Deuteronomy, chapter 28, verses 1-14 to find out many of the blessings that I have poured out on you because you are My child.

When you begin to understand My desire to bless you (or empower you to prosper) in every area of life, you will begin to see that money is really just the smallest portion of prosperity. You can have plenty of money, but be sick and so you are not prosperous in your body. Or you can be healthy but be broke and therefore not be prosperous in your finances. Or you can have money and health but your marriage may be a wreck, so you still lack total prosperity.

I have designed My Word so that every one of My children can operate in the fullness of the blessing that I desire for them through the principles of sowing and reaping. There is a lot of confusion in the church about sowing and reaping and the principles of prosperity laid out in My Word, particularly concerning financial prosperity. Many people think that poverty is My plan for My children to keep them humble. Others take the opposite approach and say that money is just supposed to fall out of trees. With so many conflicting opinions floating around, it can be difficult to know what to believe. Let's go to My Word and gain insight about what I say about prosperity so you can have true understanding.

My child, in order to understand My concepts of prosperity, let's examine the controversial subject of money and tie it back into the concept of total prosperity through sowing and reaping. It stands to reason that if I want you to be prosperous in every way, then I want you to be prosperous in your finances. My Word says that I have given you the ability to produce wealth so that you can confirm My covenant. My Word also says that My blessing brings wealth. My blessing is on you, so that blessing is designed to bring wealth into your finances.

Notice that My Word says that you have been given the power to get wealth. Money does not just fall out of the sky in bags, and the person with the most faith gets the biggest bag. I have some bad news for you. You can believe that there is going to be a bag with a million dollars in the trunk of your car tomorrow, but unless I have told you it will be there, then it won't. Sowing and reaping does not work like that. If you will operate My Word correctly, then I will bring financial abundance or wealth into your life, but it will be through a process.

Let's look first at the purpose for having the power to get wealth; it is that you may confirm My covenant. Jesus said it this way" "Seek first his (Daddy's) kingdom and his (Daddy's) righteousness, and all these things will be given to you as well" (Matthew 6:33). The first key to financial prosperity is having a heart that is pure before Me. I can see right into your heart, and I know your motives. Your motive for wanting wealth and prosperity should be that you want to establish My covenant in the earth. It is not wrong for you to partake of the abundance that I will funnel through you, but greediness for yourself cannot be your motivation on the road to true prosperity.

Now, let's look at what I mean by the power to get wealth. I did not say that wealth will just fall out of the trees. I have empowered you to obtain it because of My covenant blessing on your life. Let Me give you an example that will help to explain what I mean. Imagine a farmer with a garden. When spring comes, it's time to plant the crops. After the crops are planted, the farmer has to care for them, water them, and weed them until the time for the harvest comes.

After he has labored all summer, the time comes to gather in the harvest. How much harvest do you think he would have if he threw his seed on the ground and then sat on the porch and waited for his harvest to come? When the harvest season comes, he is going to be very disappointed, because he will have little, if any, harvest from that crop. He must properly operate the principles of sowing and reaping in order to receive his harvest.

The principles work the same for bringing prosperity, or harvest, into every area of your life, including your finances. Many people teach that all you have to do is sow your seed (offering) in the plates and that a multiplied harvest will come forth, but as I have shown you, there is more to it than that. You have to care for the seeds that you sow if you are to reap a harvest from them. You must begin to seek Me to guide you into the harvest that you desire.

For example, if you sow and believe for a better job, then you need to show yourself to be the most promotable employee on your company's payroll. If you are sowing for your business to grow, then you must do everything you know to do to make it succeed, and seek Me to show you how to prosper it in ways you never thought possible. The cycle of sowing and reaping is that you plant, labor, and then harvest.

What should the farmer in our example do? He should trust Me for a tremendous harvest from his crop. He should then begin seeking My wisdom to be the best farmer he can be to reap that harvest. Then he should prepare his field, sow his seed, and do everything he knows to do to bring about that harvest. My blessing will be on him as he labors, and his harvest will be according to his faith and diligent effort. My child, like the farmer, you must do your part or else you will see very little harvest come back on the seeds that you sow.

Sowing and reaping extend far beyond giving your money to receive a harvest. Financial prosperity really is the smallest part of the big picture of whole life prosperity I have provided for you. You must learn that My Word operates off the principles of sowing and reaping in receiving anything from Me. I sowed My Son to receive you as My child. Your seed can be anything. You sow your faith and time in prayer to receive a harvest of the answers to your requests. You can sow your time, your talent and abilities, your treasure, your love, faith, etc. believing for a harvest according to My Word. For example, if you wanted to be a great guitar player, then you would sow your time and energy into learning to play, believing Me to bless the seed that you were sowing and multiply your efforts by My anointing.

My child, I desire to bring abundant manifestation of blessing into your life, and I am able to do it through the purity of your heart, and through your diligence to sow and do your part until you reap the harvest. Sow greatly, my child, and I will prosper you greatly in every area of life. I love you!

Love,

Dad

Words from the Father's Heart

Deuteronomy 28:1-13—"If you fully obey the LORD your God (Daddy) and carefully follow all his commands I give you today, the LORD your God (Daddy) will set you high above all the nations on earth. All these blessings will come upon you and accompany you if you obey the LORD your God (Daddy): You will be blessed in the city and blessed in the country. The fruit of your womb will be blessed, and the crops of your land and the young of your livestock—the calves of your herds and the lambs of your flocks. Your basket and your kneading trough will be blessed. You will be blessed when you come in and blessed when you go out.

"The LORD (Daddy) will grant that the enemies who rise up against you will be defeated before you. They will come at you from one direction but flee from you in seven.

"The LORD (Daddy) will send a blessing on your barns and on everything you put your hand to. The LORD your God (Daddy) will bless you in the land he is giving you. The LORD (Daddy) will establish you as his holy people, as he promised you on oath, if you keep the commands of the LORD your God (Daddy) and walk in his ways. Then all the peoples on earth will see that you are called by the name of the LORD (Daddy), and they will fear you. The LORD (Daddy) will grant you abundant prosperity—in the fruit of your womb, the young of your livestock and the crops of your ground—in the land he swore to your forefathers to give you.

"The LORD (Daddy) will open the heavens, the storehouse of his bounty, to send rain on your land in season and to bless all the work of your hands. You will lend to many nations but will borrow from none. The LORD (Daddy) will make you the head, not the tail. If you pay attention to the commands of the LORD your God (Daddy) that I give you this day and carefully follow them, you will always be at the top, never at the bottom."

Proverbs 10:22—"The blessing of the LORD (Daddy) brings wealth, and he adds no trouble to it."

Deuteronomy 8:18—"But remember the LORD your God (Daddy), for it is he who gives you the ability to produce wealth, and so confirms his covenant, which he swore to your forefathers, as it is today."

Matthew 6:33—"But seek first his kingdom and his righteousness, and all these things will be given to you as well."

Luke 6:38—"Give, and it will be given to you. A good measure, pressed down, shaken together and running over, will be poured into your lap. For with the measure you use, it will be measured to you."

Ephesians 3:20-21—"Now to him who is able to do immeasurably more than all we ask or imagine, according to his power that is at work within us, to him be glory in the church and in Christ Jesus throughout all generations, for ever and ever! Amen."

Philippians 4:19—"And my God (Daddy) will meet all your needs according to his glorious riches in Christ Jesus."

Isaiah 48:17 NKJV—"Thus says the LORD (Daddy God), your Redeemer, the Holy One of Israel: 'I am the LORD your God (Daddy), who teaches you to profit, who leads you by the way you should go.'"

Questions from the Father's Heart

1) How has this letter impacted your understanding of the word "blessing" and its meaning in your life? ____________

____

____

____

____

____

2) What are some areas that you and those you love have lacked My whole life prosperity? ____________________

____

____

____

____

____

3) How are you going to begin to work the principles of sowing and reaping I have taught you in this letter like the diligent farmer caring for his crops? ______________

____

____

____

____

____

4) What do you have that you can sow into My Kingdom to reap a bountiful harvest? (Hint: time, talents, abilities, prayers, etc.)______________________________

____

____

____

____

____

Prayer to the Father

Daddy,

Thank You so much for making provision for me to have prosperity in every area of my life. I am grateful to You for teaching me the principles of sowing and reaping so that I can begin to apply them to my life. Please show me different kinds of seed I have right now that I can begin to sow believing for a multiplied harvest. Please help me to be a diligent sower so I can reap a tremendous harvest. Please help me to care for the seeds I sow into Your Kingdom according to Your Word. I believe that I receive a bountiful harvest on every good seed that I sow. I love You! In Jesus' name I pray.

Love,

____

Identifying with My Father

My Heavenly Daddy has empowered me to prosper in every area of life so that I have abundance in all things.

(Now, add your own thoughts.)

Letter #27:

Dealing with the Devil

Dear ____,

(your name here)

As I begin the final letter in the teachings on "Kingdom Principles," I want you to understand My great love for you. My power and ability have given you everything you need for life and Godliness. You must understand that it is not enough just to know how to operate according to My Kingdom laws and principles. You must also know how to combat the forces of darkness that would try to steal, kill, and destroy in your life. This letter will teach you how to deal with the enemy and enjoy the victory over him and his works that Jesus obtained in His death on the cross.

The devil has been man's enemy since the beginning of time. He hates Me, and he hates you because you are made in My image. When Adam sinned in the garden, Satan became the god of the world. My Word tells you to beware of him because he "prowls around like a roaring lion looking for someone to devour" (1 Peter 5:8). Before you received My gift of salvation, you were part of the enemy's kingdom and were subject to his rule and dominion over you. Now, by accepting the work that Jesus did for you on the cross, you have been delivered from the kingdom of darkness and have been made a part of My Kingdom. You are no longer subject to the enemy or to his work in your life. The blood of Jesus Christ has redeemed you from the devil's dominion.

My child, in order to understand how to apply the victory that you have been given over the enemy, let us return once again to the vision of My throne room. Remember that you are clothed with a royal robe of righteousness and are seated on a throne at Jesus' right hand. According to My Word, you have been given authority through Christ over ALL the power of the enemy. Remember, I taught you in the letter concerning your position in Christ that if you use your authority, NOTHING will in any way harm you.

Now remember something that you know the enemy has done in your life. How did he go about accomplishing his goal? He was sneaky. He did not walk up to you and say, "I'm the devil, and I am about to do so-and-so to you." Of course he didn't! Since you are My child, he no longer has any legal right to operate in your life. You have all authority over him and his works in your life, and he knows it. The only way that he can work in your life is to get you not to exercise your authority over him, and thus leave him free to work. My Word is spiritual law, and it states that the enemy has no right to work in your life. However, the forces of darkness are outlaw spirits, and they will not obey spiritual law unless you force them to with the authority of the name of Jesus.

As we return to the image of My throne room, imagine Me saying to you, "My child, the enemy is going to attack you today. He is going to come at you with such and such. He will speak this lie and that lie to you, but always remember that he is the father of lies and there is no truth in him.

Refuse to believe him or even listen to his lies. Use the authority that I have given you in the name of Jesus to run him out of your life."

Now, picture a silly looking little demon walking into My throne room with a little bag of lies over his shoulder. What would you do about him? You would cast him and his silly bag of lies out of your life in the name of Jesus. When you put the name of Jesus on your lips, he would grab his little bag and run away as fast as his legs would carry him. I know this may seem like a silly example, but if you will begin to rightly see the enemy in the light of My Word, then his works will seem just as silly to you as this example. He is powerless and defeated.

The adversary's only ability in your life is what you allow him to have. How is this possible? Remember the teaching from the letter about your position in Christ? The authority that Jesus had when He walked the earth has been given to you to exercise. I cannot exercise that authority on your behalf because I have given it to you. Remember the illustration of the father giving his teenager the new car? My child, I will be glad to help you take your place in exercising what is rightfully yours in Christ, but I cannot do it for you. Ask My Holy Spirit to strengthen you and help you use your authority over the wicked one. My child, use your authority and run the devil out of your life for good. He has to go when you stand in the authority of the name of Jesus. I love you and I will always help you.

Love,

Dad

Words from the Father's Heart

John 10:10—"The thief comes only to steal and kill and destroy; I have come that they may have life, and have it to the full."

James 4:7—"Submit yourselves, then, to God (Daddy). Resist the devil, and he will flee from you."

2 Peter 1:2-4—"Grace and peace be yours in abundance through the knowledge of God (Daddy) and of Jesus our Lord. His divine power has given us everything we need for life and Godliness through our knowledge of him who called us by his own glory and goodness. Through these he has given us his very great and precious promises, so that through them you may participate in the divine nature and escape the corruption in the world caused by evil desires."

1 Peter 5:8—"Be self-controlled and alert. Your enemy the devil prowls around like a roaring lion looking for someone to devour."

Ephesians 6:10-18—"Finally, be strong in the Lord and in his mighty power. Put on the full armor of God (Daddy) so that you can take your stand against the devil's schemes. For our struggle is not against flesh and blood, but against the rulers, against the authorities, against the powers of this dark world and against the spiritual forces of evil in the Heavenly realms. Therefore put on the full armor of God (Daddy), so that when the day of evil comes, you may be able to stand your ground, and after you have done everything, to stand. Stand firm then, with the belt of truth buckled around your waist, with the breastplate of righteousness in place, and with your feet fitted with the readiness that comes from the gospel of peace. In addition to all this, take up the shield of faith, with which you can extinguish all the flaming arrows of the evil one. Take the helmet of salvation and the sword of the Spirit, which is the word of God (Daddy). And pray in the Spirit on all occasions with all kinds of prayers and requests. With this in mind, be alert and always keep on praying for all the saints."

Questions from the Father's Heart

1) How has this letter opened your eyes regarding how to deal with your enemy effectively? ____________________

____

____

____

____

____

____

2) What are some areas that you can identify in your life and in the lives of your loved ones where the enemy has been at work? ______________________________

____

____

____

____

____

____

3) How are you going to begin to implement what you have learned to combat the forces of darkness? ____________

____

____

____

____

____

____

PRAYER TO THE FATHER

Daddy,

I love You, and I am grateful to You for teaching me about how to walk in victory over the enemy. I realize that he has been at work in my life and in the lives of those I care about. Help me to be sober and vigilant according to Your Word so that he does not steal, kill, or destroy in our lives. Help me to use my authority and Your armor to walk in victory over the wicked one. Help me to see right though every one of his works and not listen to even one of his lies. I love You, and I thank You that I have the victory. In the name of Jesus I pray.

Love,

____

Identifying with My Father

As I exercise my authority in Jesus' name over the enemy and his works, he runs from me in terror!

(Now, add your own thoughts.)

Letter #28:

The Father's Purpose for You

Dear ______________________________,

(your name here)

I love you, and I have laid out a good plan for your life. This plan is the course that I have set out for your life to follow, and if you are to live a life filled with satisfaction and fulfillment, it is necessary that you know it and follow it. My child, it is My pleasure to reveal My plan and directions to you. This letter will teach you how to receive My vision for your life and My directions to accomplish the vision I give you.

In order to understand My vision for your life and receive My directions, you must first understand My divine plan. My child, you were set apart (consecrated) for a specific path, plan, and destiny before you were born. As I have told you many times in these letters, My plan for you is a good plan that will lead to wholeness and prosperity in every area of your life.

As I reveal My plan for your life to you, it becomes your vision or the picture of the path that your life is to follow.

This vision will not show you where you are now, but will show you where I have for you to go. I will not reveal My entire plan for you all at once because you would be too overwhelmed. I will reveal it to you a piece at a time as you are prepared to receive it. My child, there will be many steps in between where you are now and the place I reveal to you that we are going, but rest assured that I will guide you all the way.

Let Me illustrate how the vision and instructions that I give you work together to bring you into My plan and purpose for your life. Let's pretend that you wanted to build your dream house. First, you would start with a picture of what you wanted the house to look like. This would be your vision. Then you would need a set of instructions to take you from a big pile of building materials to the finished product. This set of instructions would be called a blueprint. It is the step-by-step plan for you to build that dream house that you want to live in. Only if you follow the blueprint exactly will your house look like the one in your picture.

My child, in the same way that you would build this house, you must build your life based on the instructions that I will give you to carry out the plan (vision) that I have for you. If you have a vision but no instructions, then all you have is a dream. If you have instructions but no vision, then you will be in bondage to dogma. Only when the two are coupled together is there a complete plan for the work that I have for your life, and the combination of vision and the instructions to carry out that vision is My divine direction for your life.

My child, many people think that receiving My divine direction is difficult, but please allow Me to show you how simple it is to receive it. Return in your mind to the vision that I gave you of the two of us walking together as a Father and child. Do you remember the letter where I taught you how to hear My voice? As you continue to make the lessons I taught you a part of your daily life, you will walk in closer and closer fellowship with Me, and you will be better prepared to receive the plan and instructions that I have for you.

Receiving My plan and instructions for your life is as simple as imagining the two of us together in our quiet place. You are My small child, and I am your Daddy holding you by the hand. You need to simply ask Me like a child to reveal My plan and instructions to you in My time. I will be glad to grant your requests for you. My child, be sure to get a notebook and write down your requests for My plans. Also, write down the things that I show you, the vision and the instructions that I give you. These, along with My Spirit, will guide and direct you in the paths that I have laid out for you.

My child, My Word says that I will give you the desires of your heart. I have placed desires in every person's heart. Those desires are the seeds of the destiny that I have laid out for you. As you grow in your relationship with Me and surrender more and more to the work of My Spirit in your life, these desires that I have placed in you will come into sharper focus, and I will fulfill these desires, because I have placed them inside you. My plan and My instructions will teach you how to receive and walk in the things that I have placed in your heart.

My child, receiving My instructions is not hard or difficult. You simply need to ask Me for them, knowing that I will gladly give them. When I give you vision and instruction, you need to be diligent to obey what I have shown you to do. Faithfulness is being found doing the last thing I told you to do. You must continue to be faithful and obedient to walk in the fullness of what I have for you.

Let Me illustrate the importance of obedience with a simple example. Suppose that you were helping a child make a batch of cookies. You know that you have to follow the recipe exactly if the cookies are to turn our correctly. You are reading the recipe and instructing the child as to what ingredients to get out of the cabinets to put in the bowl for the cookies. Suppose the child asks you what to do next, and you say, "Please go get the sugar." Well, the little child goes off and gets distracted and comes back five minutes later and asks you what needs to be done next. You reply, "We still need the sugar. Can you get it, please?" Because you are reading the recipe, you know that you cannot proceed to make a successful batch of cookies without the sugar. Until the child gets the sugar out of the cabinet so it can be added to the mix, there is no need for you to provide further instruction.

My child, many times My children do the same thing. They ask Me what to do, I tell them, and they don't follow through. When they come back to Me wanting further instructions for their lives, I will point them back to the last thing I told them to do because everything I instruct them to do is all part of the process. It is imperative that you obey Me when I tell you to do something so that the recipe of your life will turn out to be what you want.

My child, I love you, and it is My pleasure to lead and guide you in the paths of life. If you will receive My direction and follow it, then I promise that your life will turn out to be happy and prosperous. I love you, My child, with all My heart.

Love,

Dad

Words from the Father's Heart

Jeremiah 1:5—"Before I formed you in the womb I knew you, before you were born I set you apart; I appointed you as a prophet to the nations."

Jeremiah 29:11—"'For I know the plans I have for you,' declares the LORD (Daddy), 'plans to prosper you and not to harm you, plans to give you hope and a future.'"

Psalm 32:8—"I will instruct you and teach you in the way you should go; I will counsel you and watch over you."

Hebrews 12:1-2—"Therefore, since we are surrounded by such a great cloud of witnesses, let us throw off everything that hinders and the sin that so easily entangles, and let us run with perseverance the race marked out for us. Let us fix our eyes on Jesus, the author and perfecter of our faith, who for the joy set before him endured the cross, scorning its shame, and sat down at the right hand of the throne of God (Daddy)."

Isaiah 55:8-9—"'For my thoughts are not your thoughts, neither are your ways my ways,' declares the LORD (Daddy). 'As the heavens are higher than the earth, so are my ways higher than your ways and my thoughts than your thoughts.'"

Romans 8:32—"He who did not spare his own Son, but gave him up for us all – how will he not also, along with him, graciously give us all things?"

Luke 12:32—"Do not be afraid, little flock, for your Father (Daddy) has been pleased to give you the kingdom."

Psalm 37:4—"Delight yourself in the LORD (Daddy) and he will give you the desires of your heart."

Questions from the Father's Heart

1) What has this letter taught you about the plan that I have for your life and how to receive it? ____________________

____

____

____

____

2) What have I shown you to this point that you feel is part of My plan and direction for you? ____________________

____

____

____

____

3) What are the desires that you have deep in your heart?

____

____

____

____

____

4) What things do you know that I have instructed you to do that you have not followed through on as well as you could? ____________________

____

____

____

____

5) How will you begin to implement the principles I have taught you in this letter to receive My complete plan and direction for your life on a daily basis? ____________________

____

____

____

____

Prayer to the Father

Daddy,

Thank You so much for making a good plan for My life and being willing to share it with me. Please reveal to me Your vision for my life. Make clear to me the plans that You have for me. Please give me the specific instructions that I need to bring Your plan to pass. I know they will be many, but I am listening. Help me to hear from You daily and not miss a single one. As You give me Your direction for my life, I will be diligent to obey You every step of the way with Your help. I trust You that as I hear from Heaven and walk in Your plan, my life will be filled with success, peace, and confidence. I love You! In Jesus' name I pray.

Love,

____

Identifying with My Father

My Heavenly Daddy instructs me and holds me by the hand as He leads me down the path that He has prepared for me to walk. *(Now, add your own thoughts.)*

Letter #29:

Living Free from Fear

Dear ______________________________,

(your name here)

My love for you is so great that it is more than you can even imagine. My love for you is perfect in every way. I always have your best interest at heart in all things. In the many letters that I have written to you so far, I have taught you many things to help you succeed in My Kingdom. You are a strong, Godly child, and I am very proud of you. Today I want to further help you succeed by uncovering the greatest tool that your enemy tries to use against you: fear!

Fear can take many different forms, and its most basic definition is believing anything that is contrary to My Word. It is the negative application of the faith that I have given you. When you believe anything that you see, hear, think, etc. that is contrary to what My Word says about your situation, you step into fear at that moment. My child, when you begin to see everything as either trust in My Word or trust in something contrary to My Word, you will realize that most people's lives are filled with fear.

Fear is not necessarily being scared silly by watching a scary movie, but it can be. Fear can be as simple as worry over losing your job, or not being able to make your house payment. Worry is simply a manifestation of fear. My child, begin to examine your life, your thoughts, and your words. Then begin to measure what you are thinking and saying against what My Word says. For example, think about the last time you said something like, "I think I am coming down with a cold," or "It seems that something is always stealing my money." Statements like these made from fear are not in line with My Word, because My Word promises you health and prosperity.

In the letter on faith, I taught you that faith is simply the ability to believe, and that you are responsible for forming the faith I have given you into belief in My Word. Let's call the application of your faith into trust in My Word "faith," and let's call trust in the ability of the enemy "fear." Now, we have two words to easily describe trust and belief in both kingdoms. My child, according to My Word, there are only two kingdoms, and every thought, word, and action must be made according to the principles of one kingdom or the other. My Kingdom is built on "faith," or trust in My ability. The kingdom of the world is built on "fear," or trust in the enemy's ability.

Fear is a force that paralyzes you because it hinders My ability from flowing freely in your life. I will illustrate this truth with the following example. Imagine a dark room where you can see nothing. Now, imagine that you turn on the light switch, and all of a sudden you can see everything clearly. Now, turn the switch back off, and again you can see nothing. The example illustrates the relationship between faith and fear. Faith is the light, and fear is the darkness. Just like there can be no darkness where there is light, there can be no fear where there is faith. Faith and fear, like light and dark, are mutually exclusive. You can have one or the other, but not both.

My child, let Me give you another example that will begin to teach you fear's place in the life of a child of faith. Pretend that you are the child of an earthly king, and that you work together with your father, the king, in handling the affairs of the kingdom. Let's imagine that he has given all authority over kingdom matters to you so that when you speak, it is just like him speaking.

One day a message comes to the throne room saying that a plot to kidnap you and the king to hold you for ransom has been discovered, and that the would-be kidnappers are at a house down the road making preparations. As a child of the king with the rights to command as the king, what are you going to do? Are you and the king going to go into hiding for fear of what might happen? Of course not! You would command soldiers to go at once to arrest the guilty parties and throw them in jail! My child, I know this example seems silly, but so does acting in fear when you begin to understand who you are as My child.

How does this example help you begin to deal with fear? Remember that you are seated with Me in My royal throne room. When anything faces you that is contrary to My Word, you have a choice to make. Are you going to act on My Word in "faith," or are you going to embrace something that contradicts My Word and act in fear?

Now, My child, let's look at some practical steps to dealing with fear in your life. First of all, you must deal with fear from the perspective of a royal child seated in My throne room with authority. You must renew your mind to what My Word says in all things, because as you do, you will come to know My love, which will cast out all your fear. Your mind can only dwell on one thought at a time, so you must begin to be aware of what you think from moment to moment. Begin to examine your every thought, word, and action against My Word and if it does not line up, then eliminate it from your life.

This is not a process that happens overnight, because faith, like fear, is a lifestyle. I have taught you about your authority as My child. You must speak to fear and command it to leave your life. Command it to leave and stop coming into your mind just like you would give the order to have the kidnappers arrested in the example I gave you.

You also need to begin to take heed what you watch and what you hear. As you grow and mature, you will find that the world is so full of fear that it is constantly bombarding you at all times. My child, you cannot expect to put the world and its system into your life all day every day and be able to walk in faith. It does not work like that. Just like bodybuilders prepare for competition by being disciplined and diligent in their exercise and eating habits every day, so you too must prepare for success and faith by your daily habits.

My child, ask the Holy Spirit to help you overcome all fear in your life. Ask Him to help you be careful to guard yourself so that you are not constantly feeding on things that are contrary to My Word. He will be glad to help you every minute of the day. I love you with all My heart.

Love,

Dad

Words from the Father's Heart

2 Timothy 1:7—"For God (Daddy) did not give us a spirit of timidity, but a spirit of power, of love and of self-discipline."

Matthew 6:25-33—"Therefore I tell you, do not worry about your life, what you will eat or drink; or about your body, what you will wear. Is not life more important than food, and the body more important than clothes? Look at the birds of the air; they do not sow or reap or store away in barns, and yet your Heavenly Father (Daddy) feeds them. Are you not much more valuable than they? Who of you by worrying can add a single hour to his life?

"And why do you worry about clothes? See how the lilies of the field grow. They do not labor or spin. Yet I tell you that not even Solomon in all his splendor was dressed like one of these. If that is how God (Daddy) clothes the grass of the field, which is here today and tomorrow is thrown into the fire, will he not much more clothe you, O you of little faith? So do not worry, saying, 'What shall we eat?' or 'What shall we drink?' or 'What shall we wear?' For the pagans run after all these things, and your Heavenly Father (Daddy) knows that you need them. But seek first his kingdom and his righteousness, and all these things will be given to you as well."

1 John 4:15-18—"If anyone acknowledges that Jesus is the Son of God (Daddy), God (Daddy) lives in him and he in God (Daddy). And so we know and rely on the love God (Daddy) has for us. God (Daddy) is love. Whoever lives in love lives in God (Daddy), and God (Daddy) in him. In this way, love is made complete among us so that we will have confidence on the day of judgment, because in this world we are like him. There is no fear in love. But perfect love drives out fear, because fear has to do with punishment. The one who fears is not made perfect in love."

Psalm 27:1—"The LORD (Daddy) is my light and my salvation – whom shall I fear? The LORD (Daddy) is the stronghold of my life – of whom shall I be afraid?"

Psalm 3:3-6—"But you are a shield around me, O LORD (Daddy); you bestow glory on me and lift up my head. To the LORD (Daddy) I cry aloud, and he answers me from his holy hill. I lie down and sleep; I wake again, because the LORD (Daddy) sustains me. I will not fear the tens of thousands drawn up against me on every side."

Questions from the Father's Heart

1) What areas of your life have you been operating in fear?

____

____

____

____

____

2) How has fear kept you from walking in My Word? ______

____

____

____

____

3) What are some ways you can think of to begin to eliminate fear from your life? ______________________

____

____

____

____

4) What is your plan of action to daily reject fear and its operation in your life, and to embrace My Word as your firm foundation? ______________________

____

____

____

____

PRAYER TO THE FATHER

Daddy,

Thank You so much for revealing the tool of the enemy to me. I realize that I have let fear work in my life in many ways. Help me not to worry or be fearful about anything. Please help me to reject all fear and to use Your Word to make the foundation of my life firm. In Jesus' name, I reject all fear. I command it to leave my life and mind as though it were never there. I do not fear because I rest on my Heavenly Father's promises. I thank You, Daddy, that I am fear—free. In Jesus' name I pray.

Love,

____

Identifying with My Father

Fear has no place in me because I am at rest in my Heavenly Daddy's love. *(Now, add your own thoughts.)*

Letter #30: Victory Over Depression

My Dearest Child ____________________________,

(your name here)

You are the song in My heart, and My love for you is like a beautiful melody. Receive and rest in My love today. My child, your enemy and the world's system desire to steal your joy and the song that I have placed in your heart. Heaviness and depression are the enemy's tools used to spread a black cloud over your life. Let's learn together today how to conquer these works of the wicked one.

My child, depression is a foul work of the devil. Sometimes he uses a circumstance to bring this heaviness on, and other times it seems that depression can just settle in out of the clear blue sky. Either way, depression and its twin, oppression, are simply works of the enemy designed to throw your life and your relationship with Me out of focus. Your enemy knows that if he can do this, then he can slow or even stop your spiritual forward progress. Let Me teach you how to deal with these tools of the enemy and walk in victory over them.

My child, return with Me to the vision of My throne room that I shared with you in the letter on your position in Christ.

Picture yourself there at Jesus' right hand just like My Word says. Now, imagine that a little bitty demon comes walking into My throne room carrying a box. He walks right up to your throne, sits his little box down, opens it up, and out comes an ugly black cloud. That black cloud moves up and settles right around your head so that you can't even see your hand in front of your face. This black cloud represents the works of the enemy called depression and oppression.

My child, in this situation what would you do about this black cloud? Would you just sit there and allow My glory to be blocked from your life by this work of the enemy? Would you fall off your throne and roll around on the ground crying? Of course not! You would do exactly as I have taught you to do! Visualize yourself standing up from your throne and saying in a loud voice, "In the name of Jesus, you demon and you black cloud of depression, leave me now!" Picture that little demon screaming in terror, grabbing his box, running as fast as he can from the throne room, and the black cloud simply disappearing into thin air. Now, what would you do? My Word says that I have given you a garment of praise for the spirit of heaviness. You would begin to sing and praise Me for your deliverance through the name of Jesus.

This simple example illustrates how you must deal with the enemy and his work of depression. I have given you a garment of praise to wear, not a spirit of despair or heaviness. Anytime you feel any heaviness, oppression, or depression beginning in your mind or heart, you must be diligent to speak to it and deal with it just like I have shown you in this illustration. Otherwise, it can dominate and rule your life like it does so many people's lives. You must continue to exercise your authority over the wicked spirits and their depression and praise Me until all heaviness is gone. It may not leave the first time you speak to it, but keep commanding it to leave and it will go.

The garment of praise is worn by belief. When you feel heavy, begin to praise Me, and the heaviness will have to leave. You wear the garment of praise by opening your mouth and letting the praise come out. You must actively put it on just like you get up and put on a shirt every morning. Just because you own shirts does not mean that you are wearing one. A shirt only covers you and provides comfort if you put it on and wear it. The same is true with the garment (shirt) of praise. You own it because I gave it to you, but if you don't put it on and wear it, then it does not do you any good.

My blessed child, I love you so very dearly. If you will look to My Holy Spirit for help, and be diligent to do the things I have written in this letter, then you will walk in victory over depression. You possess victory over the enemy and his works through your big brother, Jesus. Rise up and take the victory that is yours.

Love,

Dad

Words from the Father's Heart

Isaiah 54:14—"In righteousness you will be established: Tyranny will be far from you; you will have nothing to fear. Terror will be far removed; it will not come near you."

Isaiah 61:1-3—"The Spirit of the Sovereign LORD (Daddy) is on me, because the LORD (Daddy) has anointed me to preach good news to the poor. He has sent me to bind up the brokenhearted, to proclaim freedom for the captives and release from darkness for the prisoners, to proclaim the year of the LORD's (Daddy's) favor and the day of vengeance of our God (Daddy), to comfort all who mourn, and provide for those who grieve in Zion – to bestow on them a crown of beauty instead of ashes, the oil of gladness instead of mourning, and a garment of praise instead of a spirit of despair. They will be called oaks of righteousness, a planting of the LORD (Daddy) for the display of his splendor."

Colossians 1:13—"For he has rescued us from the dominion of darkness and brought us into the kingdom of the Son he loves."

Nehemiah 8:10—"Do not grieve, for the joy of the LORD (Daddy) is your strength."

Psalm 27:6—"Then my head will be exalted above the enemies who surround me; at his tabernacle will I sacrifice with shouts of joy; I will sing and make music to the LORD (Daddy)."

Hebrews 13:15—"Through Jesus, therefore, let us continually offer to God (Daddy) a sacrifice of praise – the fruit of lips that confess his name."

Questions from the Father's Heart

1) How have you reacted to the enemy's attempts to bring heaviness and depression on you in the past?__________

2) How has this letter helped you to understand how to deal with these works of darkness?

3) What will you do to apply to your life what I have taught you in this letter?

4) What are some things you can do to share My joy with others?

PRAYER TO THE FATHER

Daddy,

Thank You for teaching me how to walk in victory over the enemy's works of depression and heaviness. I recognize that You have given me victory over all his works in my life. With

Your help, I will begin to wear the garment of praise at all times, and give no place to the enemy to work in my life. In the name of Jesus, I cast off any and all depression, heaviness, and oppression. The joy of the Lord is my strength! I am delivered from all the works of darkness. Thank You for making me a joyful, praise-filled person. In Jesus' name I pray.

Love,

____

Identifying with My Father

I am clothed with the garment of praise that my Heavenly Daddy has given me to wear. *(Now, add your own thoughts.)*

Letter #31:

Freedom from Addiction

My Dear Child ______________________________,

(your name here)

Words simply cannot express My great love for you and how much you delight Me. I desire to see you free in every area of life. I have seen your struggles with addiction, and I have heard your cries to be free. In this letter I am going to teach you how to use My ability to break out of those things that have bound you and move you into the perfect liberty of Christ.

My child, I know the guilt and condemnation that you have felt as you have struggled against sin. You have felt ashamed, and these feelings have hindered our fellowship. Other believers, many of them meaning well, have made you feel as though your problem was caused by a lack of commitment and dedication. The enemy has whispered his lies into your ears telling you, "If you were really committed to God, you would stop doing this or that. If you would try harder, you would get free of that thing that is holding you bound." My child, nothing could be further from the truth!

I know that sometimes when you have struggled and been so intimately acquainted with a problem for so long, it becomes difficult to distinguish between truth and lies. Let Me give you a simple example that will illustrate for you the folly of simply trying harder and harder to obtain deliverance through your human effort.

Imagine a field that has one huge, old oak tree standing in the middle of it. It has a massive trunk and huge branches spreading out in every direction. This tree represents that root of addiction and bondage in your life. Now, imagine yourself climbing that tree with a small saw in your hand and cutting branches off here and there. Everywhere you cut one off, another one grows back. My child, cutting branches off this tree is a metaphor for trying to gain victory over bondage by simply trying harder. In this example, the harder you work at cutting the limbs off the tree, the more branches grow back.

The same is true in your life. The only way to walk in true victory is for the tree to be torn up by the roots and removed. Through His death on the cross, your big brother, Jesus, has done just that! Imagine Jesus on a huge bulldozer uprooting that tree and destroying it. In the same way, your freedom was purchased through the work that He did. Now, let Me show you how to make this truth a living reality in your life.

My child, everything that you could ever need was bought and paid for by Jesus with His own blood; however, if you don't know this or if you don't know how to access it, it does you no good. Return with Me to the example of your position in My throne room that I showed you in the letter on your position in Christ. Imagine yourself dressed in royal robes kneeling on your hands and knees before My throne. My child, there are shackles and chains binding your hands. Visualize King Jesus in all His royal splendor with the crown of the universe on His head. He stands up and moves to you; His Majesty kneels beside you and with a "click" He removes the shackles from your hands and throws the chains of bondage away.

My child, now let Me show you how to incorporate this vision into your life. You must first understand that your deliverance, like your salvation, was performed and completed on the cross. Just like salvation, you must grab hold of your deliverance by belief. I have included a prayer at the end of this letter for you to pray. Once you pray the prayer in belief, you are delivered at that moment, just like when you prayed and received your salvation. You must begin to see yourself as free just like in the vision. Refer to Letter #22 on your position in Christ, and take your rightful place as My child. Also, refer to Letter #27 on dealing with the devil, and stand on your authority in Christ to prevent him from holding you in bondage any more.

As you meditate more and more on your freedom and who you are in Christ, your actions and what you do will begin to change to line up with it. There will still be times when the old desires will return. You must be diligent to ask for My strength before they do. I am there with you by My Spirit to help you walk in victory. If you stumble, it does not mean that you are not delivered, just like when you sin, it does not mean that you are not saved. Simply ask for My forgiveness and continue to walk in who you are in Christ. The more you resist the enemy and the desires of the flesh, the less you will have to deal with the pull of those things that once held you bound. Rest in My strength, and be diligent to walk in your victory.

My child, if you will do the things that I have taught you in this letter, then your freedom will spring forth in a harvest of victory. My Spirit is with you to guide and strengthen you. Always look to Him, for He is your source. Together we will walk in the liberty that I have purposed for you. I love you, My blessed child.

Love,

Dad

Words from the Father's Heart

Galatians 5:1—"It is for freedom that Christ has set us free. Stand firm, then, and do not let yourselves be burdened again by a yoke of slavery."

John 8:44—"When he (the devil) lies, he speaks his native language, for he is a liar and the father of lies."

John 8:31-32—"To the Jews who had believed him, Jesus said, 'If you hold to my teaching, you are really my disciples. Then you will know the truth, and the truth will set you free.'"

Galatians 3:13-14—"Christ redeemed us from the curse of the law by becoming a curse for us, for it is written: 'Cursed is everyone who is hung on a tree.' He redeemed us in order that the blessing given to Abraham might come to the Gentiles through Christ Jesus, so that by faith we might receive the promise of the Spirit."

Colossians 1:13—"For he has rescued us from the dominion of darkness and brought us into the kingdom of the Son he loves."

Isaiah 61:1-3—"The Spirit of the Sovereign LORD (Daddy) is on me, because the LORD (Daddy) has anointed me to preach good news to the poor. He has sent me to bind up the brokenhearted, to proclaim freedom for the captives and release from darkness for the prisoners, to proclaim the year of the LORD's (Daddy's) favor and the day of vengeance of our God (Daddy), to comfort all who mourn, and provide for those who grieve in Zion – to bestow on them a crown of beauty instead of ashes, the oil of gladness instead of mourning, and a garment of praise instead of a spirit of despair. They will be called oaks of righteousness, a planting of the LORD (Daddy) for the display of his splendor."

QUESTIONS FROM THE FATHER'S HEART

1) Identify any areas of your life where the adversary has held you bound with addiction. ____________________

2) How has this letter helped you to understand how to deal with addiction? ____________________

3) What is your specific plan to get free and stay free of the enemy's bondage in your life?________________________

____

____

____

____

Prayer to the Father

Daddy,

Thank You that You have provided freedom from addiction through the blood of Jesus. The enemy has held me bound with ________________________ (name the things). I declare today in the name of Jesus that addiction no longer has any hold in my life. I see myself kneeling before Your Heavenly throne, and I see King Jesus removing the shackles of bondage from my life. I receive freedom from addiction this day, and I begin to walk in the perfect liberty of Christ. I bind any force of darkness and the chains that have held me bound. I stand on my authority in Christ and I break the power of addiction in my life. I am free from this moment forward, never to be in bondage to these things again. Father, please help me to continue to walk in my freedom. As You do, I will be diligent to do my best to walk in the freedom that You have provided. I love You, and I praise You for Your freedom and deliverance. In Jesus' name I pray.

Love,

____

IDENTIFYING WITH MY FATHER

I am no longer bound, for I am walking in the liberty with which Christ has set me free!

(Now, add your own thoughts.)

Letter #32:

Leaving the Past Behind

My Dear Child ______________________________,

(your name here)

I love you with an everlasting love! Oh, how I rejoiced with gladness the day that you gave your heart to Me. For so long I wanted you to become My special child, and all of Heaven celebrated the day that you accepted My free gift. Now that you are My child, you can enjoy all that I have provided for you in the covenant.

Despite your great joy to be My child, I have seen that there is often a heaviness in your heart because of the many years you feel you wasted before coming to salvation. Often, your thoughts turn backwards to the ungodly paths that you walked, the old ways you used to talk and act, etc. Your righteous heart grieves over following after selfish desires and pursuits that were in no way beneficial in the light of eternity and My Kingdom. My dearest child, what you are feeling is perfectly normal, but today I am writing to you to encourage you and to help you put this grief and lament to rest once and for all.

My child, the guilt, condemnation, and heaviness that you feel is not from Me, nor is it My plan for you. You must come to understand that you can't look forward to the future that I have for you and look back in lament at the past at the same time. Lamenting and grieving what you feel could or should have been done is both fruitless and discouraging. My child, remember Paul's words when he wrote that there was one thing he did. He said that he forgot those things that were behind him, and pressed on toward the goal to win the prize for which I had called him. He penned these words under the anointing of the Holy Spirit to instruct all My children to cut off the past, because you can't change anything or reclaim even one second of time by lamenting and feeling guilty about the past.

My child, it is true that you have wasted some of your life in following after things that are meaningless to you now, but you must recognize that guilt and condemnation over this are tools of the devil. He knows that you have lost some time in the past, and he desires to trap you into wasting your future by looking back at things that cannot be changed.

Let Me illustrate for you how counterproductive it is for you to spend your time looking back at what cannot be changed in the past. Do you remember in the first letters how I taught you to follow after Me as a small child holding his or her father's hand? I want you to return to that vision with Me so I can teach you how to cut off the past.

Imagine you and Me walking together hand in hand down a good and pleasant path. This represents the paths of life that I am trying to lead you in now as My child. Now, imagine that you keep turning away from the direction that I am leading you, first pulling in one direction and then another. As a loving Father, I keep slowing down and redirecting you so that you are going the right way. Imagine that you keep turning your head and looking back, pausing and sitting down on the ground, stumbling at times because you are not looking at the road ahead. My child, can you see how this impedes your forward progress in this example? You cannot continue to look back and keep going forward successfully at the same time.

Imagine Me as your loving Father stopping and kneeling down and looking you right in your eyes. Hear Me saying the following words: "My child, why do you keep looking back at the past as though it were still a part of your life? You are now My child in Christ; old things are passed away and all things are made new. There is no condemnation for My children. The past is gone like it never happened. I love you. Now, turn your eyes to the future, and walk with Me in the paths of life."

My child, what are you going to do now? Are you going to continue to lament and regret the past, or are you going to cut it off and move with Me into the future? Please decide to cut it off and move forward with Me. If you will trust Me and do that, I will lead you and cause the years you have remaining to be supernaturally productive and full of blessing. I can and will restore to you all that was lost if you will believe Me to do it.

As I begin to close this letter, I have something that I want you to do as a symbol that this day you have cut off all the past. First, I want you to decide forever that you are going to cut off the years that you have lost and quit wasting your future looking back in regret. Ask the Holy Spirit to help you do it, and make a decision to step out in belief that it is done. Once you have done this, I want you to get a clean piece of paper, a pen or marker, and a pair of scissors. Get alone and in your mind go to your quiet spot with Me as I taught you before. Now, think for a few minutes about the things that you regret, the bad decisions you have made, the time you have wasted, or the things that you wish you could change. As you think about these things, use your pen or marker to put marks or blotches on about one-third of your paper.

Now pray the following prayer and make this covenant with Me: "Daddy, I've made some bad choices, neglected to do some things that I should have done, done some things I regret, and feel that I've wasted some of the years that You have given me. I can't change one second of time that has passed, but today I cut off the past and I release it to You. (Cut off the marked portion of your paper and hold it up to Me.) I take You at Your Word that You have plans to bless me and give me a future and a hope. I believe You to restore to me the time that I have lost. This clean paper is a symbol of the remainder of my life, and I commit those years to you. I trust You to lead me step-by-step to make them fruitful, overflowing with abundance, and full of blessing. I know that You are able to do exceedingly abundantly above all that I can ask or think. I look forward to a blessed and productive life in You, and I do this in Jesus' name. Amen!"

My child, now take your marked paper, tear it up and put it in the trash. With this, you have cut off the past. It is gone, so no looking back! Take your clean paper that represents the life that you have committed to Me, write today's date on it, and place it somewhere you can see it when you need to be reminded of our covenant. When those thoughts of your past come back to you, be diligent to use your authority to cast them out of your mind. As you do, you will enjoy a new peace like you have never known before. I love you more than you can ever know.

Love,

Dad

WORDS FROM THE FATHER'S HEART

Romans 8:1-2—"Therefore, there is now no condemnation for those who are in Christ Jesus, because through Christ Jesus the law of the Spirit of life set me free from the law of sin and death."

Philippians 3:13-14—"Brothers, I do not consider myself yet to have taken hold of it. But one thing I do: Forgetting what is behind and straining toward what is ahead, I press on toward the goal to win the prize for which God (Daddy) has called me heavenward in Christ Jesus."

2 Corinthians 5:17-18—"Therefore, if anyone is in Christ, he is a new creation; the old has gone, the new has come! All this is from God (Daddy), who reconciled us to himself through Christ and gave us the ministry of reconciliation."

QUESTIONS FROM THE FATHER'S HEART

1) How have you spent time lamenting wasted years of your life?____

____
____
____
____

2) What steps are you going to take to keep yourself from falling back into guilt and condemnation over the past?

____
____
____
____

NOTE: Be sure to do the exercise I described in this letter and pray the prayer I have included for you!

PRAYER TO THE FATHER

Daddy,

Thank You so much for wiping out all the past when I received Jesus as my Savior and Lord. I have done as You have said, and I have cut off the past, never to look back at it again. I ask You to please restore to me the time that I have lost. Help me not to waste any more of my future by grieving over the past. I love You, and I take You by the hand today to walk into the bright future that You have for me.

Love,

____

IDENTIFYING WITH MY FATHER

I have released the past so that my Heavenly Daddy can do the new things He wants to do in my life.

(Now, add your own thoughts.)

Letter #33: Overcoming Tests and Trials

My Dear ________________________________,
(your name here)

I love you, and I always have your best interest at heart. I take great pleasure in watching you grow and mature in My Word and in My Spirit. You are the apple of My eye, and I am your proud Father. My child, I have heard your cries and seen your tears as you have undergone tests and trials at various times in your walk with Me. In your pain and sometimes frustration you have asked Me why I have allowed this or that to happen in your life. My child, today I want to help you understand both the source and the nature of the trials that assail you. I will teach you how to overcome them and walk in the victory that I have laid out for you.

My child, first and most importantly, we must establish the source of tests and trials. I am your loving Heavenly Father, and you must understand that no test or trial ever comes from Me. My Word specifically tells you not to be deceived, but that every good and perfect gift comes from Me (James 1:16-17). I wrote this specifically to tell you that there would be much misunderstanding and deception about where bad things come from, but not to listen to the lies because no bad thing is from your Heavenly Father.

Let Me give you an example that will illustrate the truth that nothing bad will come from Me or My Kingdom. Imagine a loving earthly father and his small child, very similar to the example that I gave you earlier of us together. The father loves his child so much and never wants anything bad to happen to him or her. Is that father ever going to put that child in a situation that will cause hurt or harm to teach him or her a lesson or to try to help the child mature? Of course not! He will gently guide and instruct the child in the paths that he or she should follow. This example clearly illustrates My heart toward My children as a loving Heavenly Father. I will never, ever do anything to hurt or harm one of My children in order to teach or to punish them. Jesus said it best when He said that if earthly men being evil compared to Me know how to give good gifts to their children, how much more will I, the perfect Father, give good gifts to My children (Matthew 7:11).

If no bad thing comes from Me, where then do these works that try your faith come from? My child, they come from the kingdom of darkness and its control over the world's system, but you must remember that as My child, you are delivered from the kingdom of darkness and from having to operate under the world's curse.

My child, I am the source of your strength and your deliverer. I have made a way for you to escape unharmed from every test and trial that comes your way. You must exercise your authority over the wicked one like I have taught you in order to obtain victory over his works. You have asked Me why I have allowed this or that to come against you. The truth is I have to allow whatever you allow in your life based on the authority and the responsibility that I have given to you. It is your obligation to use that authority to destroy the works of darkness against you and to walk in the victory that I have provided. Refer back to the illustration that I gave you in letter #23 on your position in Christ. In that example, tests and trials were part of the works that the enemy brought into My throne room. You have to act on My teaching and My Word to operate in your victory.

My child, I have made provision for you to walk in victory over every test and trial. Let Me show you how to obtain what I have provided. Use the example of you and Me together as a Father and child to believe Me to deliver you from each and every one of these trials and tests. You must be diligent to get to know My voice through My Word and My Spirit. I am always speaking to you, and if you are listening you will hear Me. You must then use your authority to gain the victory over the works of the enemy. Meditate on the example of your position in My throne room to learn how to use your authority. Ask the Holy Spirit to help you walk in victory over every test and trial that comes your way. I love you, My child, and I will never let you fall.

Love,

Dad

Words from the Father's Heart

James 1:16-17—"Don't be deceived, my dear brothers. Every good and perfect gift is from above, coming down from the Father (Daddy) of the heavenly lights, who does not change like shifting shadows."

John 10:10—"The thief comes only to steal and kill and destroy; I have come that they may have life, and have it to the full."

2 Corinthians 1:3-4—"Praise be to the God and Father (Daddy) of our Lord Jesus Christ, the Father (Daddy) of compassion and the God (Daddy) of all comfort, who comforts us in all our troubles, so that we can comfort those in any trouble with the comfort we ourselves have received from God (Daddy)."

Questions from the Father's Heart

1) What are some ways that the enemy has attempted to test and try you? ______________________________

____

____

____

____

2) How has this letter taught you how to deal with those works?______________________________

____

____

____

____

____

3) What is your plan to stand firm in your faith against trials and tests when they come? ______________________

____

____

____

____

____

Prayer to the Father

Daddy,

Thank You so much for delivering me from every test and trial of the wicked one. You are my Strength and my Deliverer. Thank You so much for being a loving Heavenly Father who never wants anything bad to happen to me. I trust in You and Your Word to bring me safely through any trial that should come my way. Please help me to exercise my authority over the works of darkness so that I enforce the enemy's defeat. I love you! In Jesus' name I pray.

Love,

____

Identifying with My Father

I am delivered from every evil work of the enemy thanks to my Heavenly Daddy's goodness and mercy!

(Now, add your own thoughts.)

Letter #34:

Building a Kingdom Self-Image

My Dearest Child __________________________,

(your name here)

Every letter that I have written to you, every question I have asked, and every Scripture verse I have included, have been designed to do two things: First, they have been designed to draw you into closer fellowship with Me. Second, they were designed to build into you what I call a Kingdom self-image. The first letters taught you how to have a deeper relationship with Me than ever before. Every letter since then has been aimed at accomplishing the second goal by showing you who you are in My Son, Jesus Christ. This final letter will focus on tying everything you have learned together and teaching you how to succeed in life by continuing to build your Kingdom self-image.

My child, throughout this series of letters, I have attempted to paint pictures for you of what your life is supposed to look like in Christ. I have taught you that success, health, prosperity, etc. are yours because of what your big brother, Jesus, did for you. In fact, My Word says that I have given you exceedingly great and precious promises for your success. My Word is full of promises that I have made for you—promises to put you over and bring great blessing to your life.

Unfortunately, many of My children are either ignorant or unbelieving concerning My Word, and therefore they never tap into the great blessing that I desire for them to have. My child, let Me give you an illustration of what I have done for you through Jesus. Suppose you had wanted a new car for a long time. What if one day you were to wake up and in your yard was sitting a brand-new car just like you had been wanting? What would you do? You would go outside and look at it and try to figure out how it got there. The door is unlocked so you open it up and on the seat there is a note that says, "My child, just wanted to give you something nice to bless you. The keys are in the ignition, and the title is in the dash. Love, Daddy God." What would you do? You would dance around for joy, hop in, and go for a ride enjoying the blessing that I had given you!

Let Me use the same illustration to show you what many of My children do. Imagine that you had an old, worn-out car, and all of a sudden that same brand-new car appeared in your driveway. Imagine that instead of going out to investigate the new car, you just get in your old beater and drive around the new one on the way to work. After a couple of weeks, a friend comes over and asks you who owns that new car sitting in your driveway. You reply, "I don't know, but it's not mine. Nobody would ever give me anything that nice." Your friend replies, "Well, it has to belong to someone. I'm going over and check it out." He opens the door, finds the note, and yells at you to come look because somebody has given you a brand-new car. If he had not opened the car and looked inside, you might never have known the car was yours because you could not believe that anyone would give you something so nice.

I know this seems like an unusual example, but it accurately illustrates how many of My children live their lives ignorant of My goodness. In My Word, I have given great promises of blessing and goodness for every area of life, yet so many people live their lives walking around My Word just like the person walking around the new car in the example. My child, allow Me to show you how to build a Kingdom self-image that will allow you to apply your faith in order to tap into everything that I have for you.

My Word says that with an unveiled face you behold the image of My glory as in a mirror, and that you are transformed into that image from one glory to the next. My child, My Word is a mirror. It reflects not who you are, but who you are supposed to be. In Christ, your spiritual eyes are opened to be able to see and understand My Word. If you will continually behold the image of what you are supposed to be according to the mirror of My Word in front of your eyes, then you will be transformed into the image that you are beholding. As you do, you will be transformed from one level of glory to the next by My Spirit. What image are you being transformed into? You are being transformed into the image of Christ, because that is My plan for you.

My child, as I have encouraged you through these many letters, you must go to My Word and find out what it says about you and your situation. Then, you must behold the image that My Word shows before your eyes until your life is transformed into that image. How do you behold the image of My Word before you? You must meditate on it over and over in your mind. As you do this, your mind will be renewed and you will begin to see yourself as My Word says.

As you meditate on My Word, it will find its way into your innermost being, your spirit. Once My Word becomes revelation in your spirit, belief is birthed, and you are able to use that belief to bring the image you are beholding into manifestation in your natural life. In order to see the natural manifestation of your belief, you must also continually put My Word in your heart, in your mouth, and in your actions. Merely speaking the Word is not enough. You must put action to what you say you believe in order for the power of your belief to be applied and bring forth a harvest of My great promises in your life.

My blessed child, if you will hear and apply the wisdom that I have given you in this letter, then you will build a Kingdom self-image that will allow your faith in Me to flow unhindered in your life. As always, ask My Holy Spirit to help you successfully build the image of yourself that you behold in My Word. I love you more than you can imagine, and I will never leave your or forsake you.

Love,

Daddy God

WORDS FROM THE FATHER'S HEART

2 Peter 1:2-4—"Grace and peace be yours in abundance through the knowledge of God (Daddy) and of Jesus our Lord. His divine power has given us everything we need for life and Godliness through our knowledge of him who called us by his own glory and goodness. Through these he has given us his very great and precious promises, so that through them you may participate in the divine nature and escape the corruption in the world caused by evil desires."

2 Corinthians 3:17-18 NKJV—"Now the Lord is the Spirit; and where the Spirit of the Lord *is*, there *is* liberty. But we all, with unveiled face, beholding as in a mirror the glory of the Lord, are being transformed into the same image from glory to glory, just as by the Spirit of the Lord."

Joshua 1:8—"Do not let this Book of the Law depart from your mouth; meditate on it day and night, so that you may be careful to do everything written in it. Then you will be prosperous and successful."

Psalm 1:1-3—"Blessed is the man who does not walk in the counsel of the wicked or stand in the way of sinners or sit in the seat of mockers. But his delight is in the law of the LORD (Daddy), and on his law he meditates day and night. He is like a tree planted by streams of water, which yields its fruit in season and whose leaf does not wither. Whatever he does prospers."

Luke 12:31-32—"But seek his kingdom, and these things will be given to you as well. Do not be afraid, little flock, for your Father (Daddy) has been pleased to give you the kingdom."

2 Corinthians 4:13—"It is written: 'I believed; therefore I have spoken.' With that same spirit of faith we also believe and therefore speak."

James 2:17—"In the same way, faith by itself, if it is not accompanied by action, is dead."

2 Timothy 3:16-17—"All Scripture is God (Daddy)-breathed and is useful for teaching, rebuking, correcting and training in righteousness, so that the man of God (Daddy) may be thoroughly equipped for every good work."

Questions from the Father's Heart

1) What has this letter taught you about building a Kingdom self-image?________________________

____

____

____

____

2) How have your eyes been opened to be able to better apply My Word to your life?____________________

____

____

____

____

3) What areas of your life can you think of that have lacked a Kingdom self-image? ______________________________

____

____

____

____

4) What will you do to begin to build a Kingdom self-image within yourself? ______________________________

____

____

____

____

Prayer to the Father

Daddy,

Thank You so much for the many promises in Your Word. Thank You that I am not the person I used to be, and that I am not the person that I am going to be. Please help me to begin to accurately view myself through the mirror of Your Word. Please help me to line my thoughts, words, and actions up with Your Word so that I can see a greater manifestation of Your promises in my life. Help me to build a Kingdom self-image so that I can enjoy Your blessing and share in the relationship that You desire to have with me. I love You. In Jesus' name I pray.

Love,

____

IDENTIFYING WITH MY FATHER

As a result of reading and meditating on these letters from my Heavenly Daddy, I am seeing myself more and more through His eyes. *(Now, add your own thoughts.)*

NOTES

NOTES

NOTES

ABOUT THE AUTHOR

Zach Bolt is a writer, teacher, and speaker who is passionate about introducing people to an intimate relationship with God the Father. Ever since his life was powerfully impacted by an encounter with God in his late teens, and then shaped again through a vision in his early twenties he has enjoyed an ever deepening, personal relationship with the Father. His vision is to share the Father's heart with others so they too can enjoy victory and fulfillment through their relationship with Him.

Zach is an ordained minister who has served in youth leadership at Redemption World Outreach Center and as youth pastor at Faith Harvest Church International. He currently serves as the music minster at Faith Harvest. He is a 2002 graduate of Furman University. He met his wife, Jessie, while she was working in Singapore. They were married in her home country, the Philippines, in 2006. Zach and Jessie currently reside in upstate South Carolina.

Additional copies of this book are available online at
www.lettersfromthefathersheart.com, Amazon.com,
or from your local bookstore.

To contact the author with prayer requests, praise reports,
to schedule a speaking engagement, or to sign up
for the *Letters from the Father's Heart* newsletter
please visit www.lettersfromthefathersheart.com.

Made in the USA